Mountain Biking

THE FUNDAMENTALS

Sven Klinge

NEW
HOLLAND

Published in Australia in 2000 by
New Holland Publishers (Australia) Pty Ltd
Sydney • London • Cape Town • Auckland

14 Aquatic Drive Frenchs Forest NSW 2086 Australia
218 Lake Road Northcote Auckland New Zealand
24 Nutford Place London W1H 6DQ United Kingdom
80 McKenzie Street Cape Town 8001 South Africa

National Library of Australia Cataloguing-in-publication data:

Klinge, Sven, 1969–
Mountain biking: the fundamentals
Includes index.
ISBN 1 86436 507 2

1. All terrain cycling. 2. All terrain bicycles. I. Title.

796.63

Commissioning Editor: Anouska Good
Editors: Julie Nekich, Jennifer Lane
Designer: Mark Thacker/Big Cat Design
Cover image: Sven Klinge
Illustrations and maps: Guy Holt
Photographs: All photographs are by the author except those on page 10,
Dean Piggott; page 21, Gerd Klinge; page 81, New Holland Image Library and
page 84, New Holland Image Library/Shaen Adey.
Reproduction: PICA
Printers: Kyodo Printing Company

CONTENTS

CONTENTS

About the author

Sven Klinge began cycling in the national parks around Sydney in 1988, and wrote his first book, *Cycling the Bush: 100 Rides in New South Wales*, a year later when he was nineteen. The title is now in its third edition, having sold nearly 15,000 copies. The other titles of his *Cycling the Bush* series, including *The Best Rides in Australia*, comprise Australia's premier mountain biking guidebooks. Sven's landscape photography has also been used in various walking guidebooks, advertisements and magazine articles.

Sven has toured extensively throughout Australia, New Zealand and Europe, but it is the great mountain wilderness world heritage areas of south-west Tasmania and Fiordland that particularly draw his attention. In addition to writing cycling books, Sven has co-authored a major national walking title on Australia's mountains with Tyrone Thomas and a camping guide with Adrian Hart. *Classic Walks of Australia*, published by New Holland, is his forthcoming project.

Educated at Sydney University, Sven currently works as a freelance writer for professional legal journals, an accountant and a contract network administrator. His website can be found at http://www.zeta.org.au/~avatar

Acknowledgments

Much appreciation to the following people, companies and organisations for their support in the publication of this guidebook: Anouska Good at New Holland Publishers; Russell Murray and Tony Young at Apollo Bicycles; John Bazzano at Shimano Australia; Fraser McLachlan and Katherine McRoberts at Macpac Wilderness Equipment; Andrew Hanna at the Land Information Centre, New South Wales; David Moss at Mountain Designs; Ian Gibson at Paddy Pallin; Grant Minervini and Guy Reynolds at Cascade Designs; Tracey Orr at AUSLIG, Canberra; Tim Campbell at Adventure Designs/One Planet/Aiking Australia; David Huxley at Berrivale Orchards (Isosport); Paul Gibbs at Maxwell (Lowepro); Sarah Moulder at Kathmandu; Greg Foord at Spelean (Sweetwater Guardian water purifiers); Robert Avery at TASMAP; Adrian Goodrich at the Department of Natural Resources and Environment, Victoria; John Lane at the South Australian Department of Environment and Natural Resources; Graham Stanton at the Queensland Department of Natural Resources; Martin Hanley at Hanley Trading; Noel McFarlane at Bunyip Bags; Fuji Film; D. Nicholls, M. Enjeti, and B. Johnston at the Tasmanian Department of Tourism; Salomon; Eddie Salas Cycles, Rooty Hill; Tom Andrews at Macson Trading Company (Avocet). I'd also like to thank my cycling companions Adrian, Cam, Carmen, Dean, Francis, Matthew, Sean and Tyrone.

Preface

Rapid development of off-road cycling technology in the last two decades, with its use of modern alloys and perpetually changing designs, means a general book on mountain biking can never claim to be 'definitive'. Two forces essentially drive advances in mountain biking. One is the need for greater strength, reliability, efficiency and comfort; the other is the bane common to all high-technology industries—change for change's sake or, in short, fashion. Manufacturers are forever developing new suspension configurations, shifting mechanisms, brake designs and frame materials, all claimed to be 'better' than the previous ones.

Accordingly, books such as this one can only claim, at best, to be a snapshot of the state of the sport at any period in time. Furthermore, as this book concentrates on the fundamentals of the sport for novice and intermediate cycling enthusiasts, it refrains from delving into an in-depth discussion on the various debates that occupy advanced riders: rapid-fire versus grip-shift, hydraulic brakes versus V-brakes, titanium versus aluminium frames, and so on.

The purpose of this guide is to serve as an introductory reference to owners of mountain bikes wishing to actually go off-road. All too often, as in the case with four-wheel drive vehicles, mountain bikes are kept on the bitumen. The owner may not know where to go or what to do if the bike breaks down. While cycling off-road is simpler than a lot of the uninitiated suppose, a set of riding, preparation, and repair skills still need to be developed. Mountain bikers must also be aware of the laws and public access issues in regard to cycling in national parks, State forests and other reserves. This guide fosters a safer, more self-reliant and considerate attitude, which will ensure that all who venture out into the wilderness will enjoy the experience.

What cannot be taught is the genuine exhilaration that accompanies the thrill of exploring new tracks, hurtling down mountain trails or just seeking out a beautiful location that might be closed to four-wheel drives and is too far for day-walkers. This is where the mountain bike comes into its own, blending fitness, the great outdoors and adventure.

Happy riding.

Sven Klinge, Sydney, 2000

Introduction

From its origins on the steep hills in Marin County, northern California, in the early 1980s, mountain biking has emerged as one of the most popular recreational activities in national parks, State forests and other public reserves.

The reasons are many. With the increasing pressures of urban society, such as longer working hours, pollution and traffic congestion, the appeal of the wilderness grows. The pioneering histories of our country have created a legacy of logging tracks, fire trails and stock routes that are now ideal thoroughfares for biking enthusiasts. On the hardware front, the accelerated evolution of the mountain bike has resulted in the most versatile, robust form of transport available. Suspension forks, aluminium frames, quick-shifting indexed gears and powerful cantilever brakes have all helped make mountain biking a safe, fun and easy activity.

The mountain bike has many advantages over walking. Much more can be seen in the same time because the rider can travel at higher speeds than the walker; the perfect compromise between enjoying the scenery and arriving at the destination as planned. More luggage can be carried in panniers, which can be positioned almost anywhere on the bike. In fact, with dual panniers correctly packed, almost three times as much food and other supplies can be carried. This allows longer trips to be planned and, in the case of an emergency, an unexpected delay in reaching your destination can be endured without panic. Plus, because of the speed and silence of the bike, the cyclist often encounters local fauna, resulting in a more enjoyable outdoors experience.

For one-day rides, those not so fit can transport the bike to a high starting point and coast all the way down. This is especially convenient when public transport connects both the beginning and end of the ride.

Mountain biking also has many advantages over road bikes. Firstly, being away from the traffic that so often makes touring uncomfortable, if not dangerous, instantly helps relieve stress. But more importantly, the greatest bane of cyclists everywhere is virtually non-existent: the headwind. Riding on national park trails with dense tree cover shelters one from all but the severest of winds.

As we begin a new century, the mountain bike will no doubt get lighter, stronger, more comfortable and cheaper, ensuring the activity isn't confined only to elite athletes and hard-core enthusiasts, but is one that the whole family can enjoy.

Portal Lookout, Glenbrook, New South Wales.

Looking out over Hartley Valley from Mt York in the Blue Mountains, New South Wales.

THE MOUNTAIN BIKE

When entering any cycling shop, it's plain to see that the mountain bike is by far the most popular type of bike sold, primarily because of its versatility. Even professional racers and tri-athletes have a mountain bike as their second bike. Cycling magazines are full of articles, reviews, and advertisements for mountain bikes, and the international competitive mountain bike racing scene has quickly culminated in an officially recognised Olympic event.

Today, the mountain bike is generally regarded as the most efficient and versatile form of transport on the planet. It can go over more types of terrain than any other mode (except walking), and requires less energy to travel between any two points. In short, the mountain bike is the ideal synthesis between human, machine and nature.

The advances in mountain biking technology have been astounding. Aluminium, titanium, magnesium and carbon fibre are replacing steel and chromoly (chrome-molybdenum) traditionally used for constructing the frame and forks. These materials are lighter, stronger and ultimately have the potential to be cheaper due to simpler manufacturing processes. High technology has also played the primary role in the rapid evolution of mountain bike components, with more efficient gear selection systems, smoother suspension and greater reliability in braking and pedalling.

This, and the popularity of the bike, has ensured that all competing manufacturers specialise their bikes to suit a variety of riders' needs. Accordingly, there is a tremendous range of mountain bikes to choose from. You can pick up an imitation mountain bike when shopping at a supermarket or department store for about $150, or you can blow $20,000 on a bike with a Porsche or other fancy European sports-car logo on it.

Features

Depending on where you live, mountain bikes can also be called 'all-terrain' bikes or 'fat tyre' bikes. Essentially, they have the following characteristics that distinguish them from racers, touring bikes, commuting hybrids, BMXs and stunt bikes:

handlebar
thumbshifter
saddle
brake lever
handlebar stem
cantilever brakes
frame
saddle clamp quick release
seat post
pedal
chainwheels
bottom bracket
front derailleur
crank
rear wheel
front fork
rear derailleur
front wheel
freewheel with sprockets

Barrington Tops scenery, New South Wales.

- thick knobbly tyres, usually of 26-inch diameter
- 21, 24 or 27 indexed gears, either by grip-shift or rapid-fire levers
- adjustable suspension, either on the front or on both wheels
- quick release wheels, brakes and seat posts for ease of use
- straight handlebars aligned perpendicular to the frame
- thick, over-sized frame tubing made from light metal alloys.

Development

Although the mountain bike boom hit the Western world in the early 1980s, its origins can be traced to the interwar years. It was in 1933 that Ignaz Schwinn introduced his Excelsior into the United States, the bicycle equivalent of the tank. It was the first production bike to come with balloon tyres and coaster-hub brakes, although it still had wide, back-swept handlebars, only one gear, and was constructed from 20 kilograms of carbon steel designed in the shape of a motorbike! Few saw its merits at the time, and its use was confined to newspaper delivery and other similar utilitarian duties.

It was 40 years later before the potential of the Excelsior was discovered. Groups of local teenagers started 'terrorising' the country backroads of

A modern fully-featured mountain bike has the ability to traverse off-road terrain as well as formed tracks.

California with motorised trailbikes. The activity was so popular, that much environmental damage was caused by the hundreds of wheels spinning in soft ground. Restrictions were consequently enforced.

Legend has it that in California, where erosion problems were particularly severe, the young enthusiasts looked to alternative means of descending steep hills fast. After many spectacular and often 'unhealthy' experiments with various models, the Excelsior was found to be one of the only bikes on which riders stood a reasonable chance of reaching the bottom with all limbs intact. Needless to say, the local bike shops couldn't keep pace with the demand for this tough bike.

The Excelsior was far from perfect, however. On one famous stretch in Marin County on the slopes of Tramalpais, the Cascades Fire Trail was so steep in its 800-metre drop that continual use of the brakes was needed during these 'bombing runs'. The coaster-hub brake had a tendency to overheat to the extent that the grease was boiled right out of the bearings and had to be repacked before the next descent.

This hill, which is now named Repack Hill, is considered the birthplace of the mountain bike, for it was here that new equipment was tested. By the process of natural selection, the bike evolved to its present form. Gary Fisher, a racer, added derailleur gears, thumb shifters, and a quick-release mechanism on the seatpost of his Excelsior so that riding *up* the hill was now possible. Indeed, he was the first man to demonstrate this feat.

The maturing of the mountain bike was facilitated by two men: Joe Breeze and Tim Neenan. They developed the frame geometry and, with Californian businessman Mike Synyard, they sold the first production mountain bike, the Specialised Stumpjumper, in 1982 for $750.

Despite a huge advertising budget, the Japanese-manufactured bike had only moderate success and it wasn't until frame-builder Tom Ritchey and mountain bike rider Charles Kelly teamed up with cycling businessman Gary Fisher that mountain biking came into its own. The conservative European manufacturers initially lagged behind America, Taiwan and Japan, but soon caught up and introduced a series of high-quality frames and innovations. The introduction of aluminium rims and nylon gum-wall tyres meant that four kilograms could be shaved off the weight of the bike. By the late 1970s, this constant refining led to the setting of production standards for serious competitors. But perhaps more importantly, they gave the bike the status that is now taken for granted: the mountain bike was no longer a device whereby some offbeat suicidal daredevils got their thrills but a respectable machine that everyone from business person to bushwalker could use.

The future

Current trends of mountain bike evolution show no sign of abating. If anything, the pace of change is accelerating. Decreasing the overall weight of the bike to below 10 kilograms without compromising its strength and reliability has been a major goal of manufacturers. In-built global position systems for navigation purposes, computers that generate telemetry and diagnose faults, antilock braking mechanisms, automatic shifting, self-tightening brakes, solar-powered accessories, and a more efficient and robust drive train are all current projects for research, development and refinement.

Like any high-technology industry, debut prices for new advances are initially high, but mass production will ensure they eventually become affordable for everyone. With Shimano having a virtual monopoly on mountain bike group-sets (the brake and gear systems attached to the frame), standardisation of componentry is another feature that will help ensure compatibility of parts into the future.

All the touring features: pannier rack, water bottles and pump.

PURCHASING A MOUNTAIN BIKE

2

For the uninitiated, the range of choice and confusing techno-jargon can make purchasing a mountain bike a harrowing experience. For those looking for their dream machine there is no simple answer. The perfect bike requires interaction between rider and machine. And that's where things get complicated.

Models

Generally, the price goes up in inverse proportion to the weight. The most expensive bikes will be the lightest—under 11 kilograms. Manufacturers such as Apollo or Avanti generally have two categories of bikes. The first is their general series for entry-level bikes and touring. These bikes typically have lower-end group-sets, cheaper suspension forks and chromoly steel frames. The second category is a race series for genuine mountain biking enthusiasts. The aluminium dual suspension models with the top group-sets are found in this category.

A trend in mountain bike sales has been to market top-end models as competition bikes, rather than touring bikes. All the brochures and advertising will boast about the racing merits of a particular model. Be aware, however, that long overnight expeditions in difficult rugged terrain while carrying panniers will generate equivalent or greater stresses on a bike than a race.

If panniers are required, make sure that the frame has the mounting provisions, as many dual-suspension models have neglected this aspect.

Alternatively, there are specialised racks that attach to the seat post and are therefore dual-suspension compatible.

As to which brand name to choose, there's one important thing to remember. Shimano dominates the group-set market and therefore you will often find identical componentry on two models that may be many hundreds of dollars different in price. This concept is the same with computers where no matter what one buys, it'll generally be powered by the same INTEL chip, so one has to think twice when paying extra for a recognised 'brand name'.

The componentry group-sets generally regarded as high quality are Shimano's XT and XTR, which comprise almost everything but the frame: that is, the brakes, gears, hubs, chain, pedals, cranks and more.

Frame size

When choosing a mountain bike, size is of crucial importance, both for safety and comfort. Make sure the pedals can be reached without stretching your toes and that the top tube can be straddled with at least 50 millimetres of crotch clearance with both feet flat on the ground. If not, get the salesperson to adjust the seat or try another frame size. Mountain bike frames come in four common sizes:

Rider Leg Length	Frame Size
70–80 cm (28–31")	43 cm (17")
81–88 cm (32–34")	48 cm (19")
89–94 cm (35–36")	53 cm (21")
95 cm$^+$ (37")	58 cm (23")

Specifications

After the frame, the next most important item to consider is the brakes. These are by far the most important safety feature on the bike and if faulty can cause serious injury, if not death. Make absolutely sure the bike cannot be moved forward when the brakes are applied. The front brake alone should prevent the bike from moving. The back brake should skid when applied separately.

The spectacular vista from Mt Buffalo in Victoria.

It is a good idea to insist on having thorn-proof tubes (66 cm x 54 mm; 26 inch x 2.125 inches) once the final selection is made. Any good bike store will fit them straight away. They cost approximately $20 each but they are definitely worth it. Ensure that they either give back the original tubes as spares or deduct them from the price.

If extensive tours are likely to be planned with the new bike, a set of panniers will be needed to provide for extra storage space. Accordingly, select a bike with a strong frame and adequate provisions (eyelets and lugs) to attach front and rear panniers. There's nothing worse than having one break during a trip.

Other accessories you will need to consider purchasing when buying a new bike include:

- a helmet
- a bidon cage for water bottles
- a mountain bike pump (ensure it fits the valves)
- a repair kit
- spare tubes (ensure the valves fit the rims)
- a computer

Crossing causeways can be done without getting your feet wet.

A dangerous feature on some cheaper mountain bikes is foam handle grips which slide off when wet. This can result in a serious accident. Beware!

Some cheaper (and sometimes even the more expensive) bikes can be fitted with very hard flat seats in an effort to save weight. The inexperienced cyclist or those with sensitive posteriors might want to upgrade to a padded gel seat, such as the various Gelflex models made by Avocet. See Chapter 3 for further details.

Lastly, if the owner is young and still growing, make sure there's plenty of travel in the seat post and head tube for future adjustment.

Price

All in all, be prepared to spend at least $500 for a new bike that will be reliable and comfortable if regular mountain biking is intended. Any less and safety will be sacrificed. There's nothing worse than walking an unrideable bike out of the wilderness along an endless flat track. If one plans to do overnight rides or venture into rugged terrain, an aluminium bike with front suspension should be the minimum considered. This will probably cost about $1000, plus another $500 for accessories such as rack, panniers, computer, helmet, repair kit, spare tubes, pump and bidons.

Dual suspension bikes are even more comfortable with greater stability, handling and braking, especially when going downhill on rocky tracks. The disadvantages include extra weight, a loss of pedalling efficiency and, of course, the price. At this level, don't be surprised to see prices starting at around the $2000 mark.

Bike shops

Try to buy from a specialised bike shop rather than a department store or general sports shop. The staff will be much more knowledgeable about the product they're selling and will be better able to deal with warranty matters. City shops might be bigger but they are generally dearer as the shop rent is being factored into the price of the bike. So stay in the suburbs and preferably local. Try a number of shops first to compare prices and the helpfulness of the staff. Remember, if the staff appear either nonchalant or pushy, they'll be the same when you take a bike there for regular servicing.

One way of telling if staff personnel are making a genuine effort to assist you is if they adjust the bike to your requirements. This means selecting the right frame size as well as adjusting the handlebar height and seat-post length. Remember, the bike should fit the rider and not the other way around. Never buy a bike on looks alone. You may have to wait an extra few days for a different frame size to be ordered in but the more enjoyable ride in the long run will be worth the wait.

If spending upwards of $1000 for a new machine, you may be able to negotiate a deal where the store throws in a few items such as a repair kit, computer or other accessories, especially if you are paying cash. This may also be a good time to negotiate a discount on a helmet.

Ensure that the bike can be taken out for a test ride first. Obviously some deposit or item of value, such as car keys or wallet, will need to be given in return. Once purchased and ridden, be sure to take advantage of the complimentary after-sales service. Gear and brake cables stretch and the chain wears in, so some adjustments will have to be done after the first few rides and before venturing out into the rough stuff.

Also ask if the bike shop will trade in the bike for a newer one some time in the future. They may pay a competitive price knowing that they sold the bike in the first place.

Buying second-hand

Having to check over a second-hand bike yourself may be a daunting prospect, especially when you don't know its history. A simple checklist will prevent even the most inexperienced novice from being ripped off:

1 Apply the brakes and try to push the bike forward. If there is movement in the handlebars, the headset in the neck is loose or worn. If it can't be tightened, do not purchase.
2 When looking from the front, with the wheels lined up straight, the back wheel shouldn't be visible. If it is, the wheels are out of line. Do not buy.
3 Check each wheel for sidewards movement. If there is any play, follow the same procedure as in 2.
4 Hold the bike up and spin each wheel. It should look like it will spin for three or four minutes. If it stops straight away, the wheel needs adjusting. Only purchase if the owner can fix this adequately.

Always test-ride a mountain bike before purchasing.

5 Try to rattle the crankcase. It should be impossible. Otherwise, do not purchase the bike under any circumstances, as this is probably quite a serious fault.

6 Test-ride the bike, changing gears and using the brakes. Does the chain stay on at extreme settings? Is application of the rear brake alone sufficient to stop on short notice? If the answer to these questions is no, offer loose change or go home.

7 Make sure that the group-set componentry can be replaced. For example, Suntour went out of business, which has meant that a lot of their parts are no longer available. The same applies for obscure rim sizes, bottom brackets, the number of spoke holes, headset measurements, etc. Compatibility of parts ensures that your bike can be easily and affordably upgraded when required.

Once purchased, take the bike to a recognised bike shop and have it overhauled. Remember to get a receipt that has the engraved bike/frame number on it. This is essential for insurance reasons and to help police identify stolen frames.

Building a custom bike

This third option is reserved for the hard-core enthusiasts. Building a custom-made mountain bike is generally an extremely expensive exercise—normally upwards of $5000. Frames can be made to specifications for exact leg lengths and/or to some specified parameters, such as tube angles, materials and accessory mounting points.

You can order your own group-set or even go to the extreme of selecting a mix from various others. This is normally done to meet a certain objective, such as building the lightest or the strongest, or the most reliable bike for racing.

Uneven terrain is best negotiated on bent knees, out of the saddle.

ACCESSORIES 3

Accessories are an important part of mountain biking. More money can be spent on them than on the bike itself. Many are necessary for intensive mountain biking but most are not.

Mountain bike fashion has progressed to such a point that manufacturers advertise countless gadgets as 'must-haves', such as titanium seat-post quick-release skewers, which supposedly give the edge over other manufacturers. As the cliché goes, there's no substitute for fitness.

Mountain cyclists commonly experience breakages. In fact, the definition of a successful trip is not only reaching the destination but not having to replace anything when returning home. Wilderness can be an inhospitable place. Extreme isolation requires methodical preparation and tough equipment.

Helmet

The debate over helmets is a controversial one. On the one hand, there's the civil liberties argument and detraction from the enjoyment of cycling and on the other hand, the safety argument and the costs to the public health system. Helmets are compulsory when riding on designated roads in Australia and New Zealand. They have saved lives and prevented serious skull fractures and brain damage. They are essentially disposable—one serious fall and a new one is required. Besides costing upwards of $100, the major complaint against them is the sweaty head when riding in hot weather. Helmet manufacturers have done a lot of research in recent years trying to increase airflow within the helmet without sacrificing safety.

Taking a break in the Blue Mountains, New South Wales.

Most modern mountain biking helmets are made from energy-dispersing, impact-absorbing expanded polystyrene (EPS) that works by crushing on impact, and therefore has to be just the right density in order to reduce a 400+ G shock (that is, 400 times the force of gravity) to under 200. If the foam is too soft it will compress too easily; if it is too hard the foam itself can damage the head during a fall or collision.

Bell is the largest manufacturer of helmets and consequently can invest a lot of time and money into research and development, such as wind-tunnel testing. Their Image II helmet weighs in at only 255 grams and has a microshell bonded to the energy-absorbing liner to protect it from everyday handling abuse.

Always try on the helmet before paying for it. Remember that any small discomfort will be multiplied many times on a long ride. Make sure it has maximum ventilation to minimise sweating, the main disadvantage of wearing a helmet. Heat dissipation for the head is of utmost importance when trying to maintain your pedalling momentum.

An important point to be aware of is the use of soft, foam, adjustable fitting pads. Research has found that the thicker the foam pads, the more pronounced is a bouncing effect that causes an additional shock to the brain. Furthermore, they can result in the helmet becoming dislodged. A helmet works at optimal efficiency when the maximum amount of surface area of the inner shell of the helmet is in contact with the head. It is important, therefore, that these foam pads be kept to a minimum. Where possible, match the shape of the helmet to the shape of the skull directly and not by the use of foam. Hence the enormous range of shapes and sizes and adjustment strap systems.

Multidensity helmets, such as the Adura LT850 and HRC Equipe, have been ranked first by American university studies for deceleration. These helmets have two densities of expanded polystyrene: a hard exterior and a thick, soft inner portion. The design disperses the impact around and across the surface of the inner shell to help eliminate shattering. There is a microshell over the outer portion that protects the helmet from normal handling bumps.

Airpumps and repair kits

Chances are a flat tyre will occur sooner rather than later. All cyclists get one eventually, no matter how cautiously they ride. Common causes are thorns, sharp rocks and glass. Hitting ledges hard can cause a blow-out as well, sometimes damaging the tyre. Punctures can also be caused internally by the end of spokes penetrating the rim liner and tube, by a faulty valve, or by incorrectly fitting a new tube so that it is pinched between the rim and tyre.

According to Murphy's Law, a flat tyre will occur in the most inconvenient spot and at the most inconvenient time. But it need not spoil your trip.

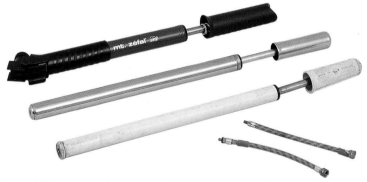

Several first-generation mountain-bike pumps. Today's models are a third of the size and don't need hoses.

Tubes vary in their size and thickness.

Contents of some typical puncture repair kits.

The correct technique in holding the pump while inflating a tube.

A portable pump and repair kit should be standard equipment on even short bike trips.

These days, MTB pumps are lightweight, small, and can be attached almost anywhere on the frame, the most common place being alongside the water bottle or on the upright tube below the seat. Make sure the pump fits the valve on the tube, as there are two types: the shraeder and presta.

Pumps, such as the popular Blackburn MP-1 Mini-pump, need no hoses and fit both valves. Despite being only 29 centimetres long, the pump is rated up to 180 psi and can inflate an average mountain bike tyre in a minute. Some airpumps, such as the Mt Zéfal Graph, have an in-built pressure gauge accurate to plus or minus 2 psi.

Pumps are also handy when needing to inflate and deflate the tyres according to the type of terrain encountered. As a general rule, the harder the surface the harder the tyre pressure and vice versa.

When selecting or putting together a puncture repair kit, make sure it includes the following items:
- patches
- glue
- tyre levers
- spare valve
- chalk
- sandpaper.

Hutchinson anti-crevaison tubes contain a self-sealing liquid for automatic sealing of small punctures. They won't however, repair tears or punctures that occur at the base of the valve.

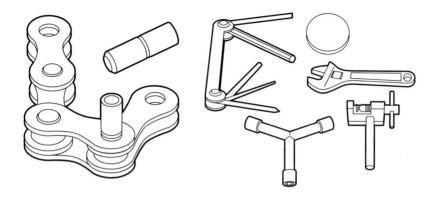

Spare links and a chain remover   *Assorted tools for extended rides.*
for chain repairs on the trail.

It is inevitable that some minor adjustments or repairs will be necessary to the rest of the bike while off-road. Although somewhat heavy, a toolkit doesn't need to be bulky and can be permanently stored in a bag under the seat or in the back pocket of one of the panniers. Some toolkits can even be encased in a dummy drink bottle and stored in a bidon cage. Standard equipment in your toolkit should include:
● puncture repair kit
● tyre levers
● Allen key set
● a small 5–10 cm shifter
● a 32 cm shifter
● multifaceted socket bone
● pliers
● screwdriver
● a 15 mm Phillips head screwdriver
● spare tube.

Some manufacturers assemble complete compact tool sets that are designed to minimise weight. These can also save on cost as individual tools, like spare parts, are usually considerably more expensive than a pre-packaged set. The saving can be as much as 50 per cent.

On longer trips, you should expand this suggested kit to include:

- spare spokes
- spoke tightening key
- chain link remover
- spare links
- grease
- small lubricating oil flask (dry molybdenum or lithium based)
- valve tightener.

Air pressure gauge

An air pressure gauge is an important part of your kit. With this gauge you can accurately measure air pressure to adjust for different riding conditions. In hot weather, or when riding in muddy conditions or sand, you should *lower* the air pressure somewhat to maximise traction. Remember, however, that low pressures over rocky terrain will increase the likelihood of punctures. On the other hand, too high a pressure will destroy any feeling of suspension the bike has, and can also lead to punctures caused by sudden impacts.

Panniers and racks

Panniers come in a wide variety of shapes, sizes and prices. What type to buy will depend on how far you intend to travel on your bike and the type of terrain. Whether carrying food, clothes, camera gear, stereo, or the wine cellar, the panniers and racks should be strong. People who make their decision solely on whether the pannier matches their bike colour are asking for trouble. Remember that if the rack-stays break, you could be forced to leave valuables behind. Other considerations besides pannier and rack strength are the strength of zippers and the number of compartments—the more the better, as gear can be sorted into different areas for ease of access. Straps at the top for a sleeping mat are convenient, as are little pockets at the back where the day's snacks and the repair kit can be stored.

A high-quality tough brand of panniers is Bunyip. Although they aren't available in the wide range of fluorescent colours that some imported brands come in, their reputation of being almost unbreakable is well founded.

Front and rear panniers can slow down progress in muddy terrain.

Designed and manufactured in Australia, Bunyip panniers are made from thick waterproof cotton stiffened by high-density polythene. The Rear Touring models have two sizeable external pockets to store toolkits, snacks, tubes, gas cookers and so on, stainless steel rack hooks that fit 8 millimetre aluminium alloy carriers, and four locking straps and adjustable shock-cords that prevent the panniers from jumping off. Large 3M reflective strips ensure safety for night riding. They are adjustable, quickly detachable, portable and have easy access to a large storage area. One pannier can hold a sleeping bag and tent in the main compartment. They come in various models of different shapes and sizes, including a handlebar mounted bag, and are available only from large specialist bike stores.

Before going on any major trip with new panniers, test them first. Put some lead ballast or bricks in them and ride up and down a few gutters. Fire trails can be very rough in places. Rocks and corrugation will cause loosely secured panniers to jump off. If they pass this test, spray them down to simulate rain. Check inside for leakage. Remember that your clothes and sleeping bag will be carried in there. If the panniers do leak—and the cheapest ones will—you can spray them with a waterproofing compound. Alternatively, simply wrap up the contents in plastic bags to keep things dry. Pack so that the items needed during the trip are on the top.

It needs to be said that there are also disadvantages with panniers:

- It is more difficult to ford deep rivers.
- There is more hassle when lowering the bike down cliffs or having to lift it over fences or other obstacles.
- A fully laden bike becomes quite strenuous to push up steep hills.
- Front panniers reduce steering manoeuvrability.
- The rider's ability to clear obstacles on the track by bunny-hopping is reduced.

There are two ways around most of these problems. The first is to purchase panniers that are easily detachable so they can be carried separately across rivers or lowered down cliffs. The second way is to use a backpack, as many bushwalkers-turned-cyclists do. Despite initial assumptions, wearing a backpack does not create any major stability problems and pushing up hills becomes much easier. Backpacks also have the advantage of better insulating gear from shocks and river crossings. You also have the ability to take gear down to a river campsite where access is often only on foot.

Panniers should be secured to the bike using a strong, lightweight rack. The premium brand that all others are based on is Blackburn.

Vehicle bike racks

Bike racks are used to transport bikes to and from staging areas. Good racks cost about $100 and accommodate three bikes. They are fitted on the tow bar of a vehicle. The bikes are secured to the rack by two plates that squeeze the frames between them and are fastened by two winged nuts. The introduction of red-light and speed cameras has resulted in the enforcement of licence-plate obstruction laws, so new racks have provisions to mount the licence plate on the back. If transporting bikes at night, you also need to fit a light on the licence plate.

Alternative bike rack designs, such as those made by Thule, can mount the bike securely on the car roof. This is a good option for four-wheel drivers who can damage their bikes along rough trails, but has the disadvantage of susceptibility to damage from overhanging branches. Another alternative is the Ark bike carrier which tilts downwards, thus allowing hatchbacks, utility trays and wagon rear doors to open. One thing to watch out for is keeping the tyres away from the hot exhaust pipe.

Tyres

Choose your tyres according to the type of terrain and the climate that you will encounter. For wet rainforest areas, wide knobbly tyres are recommended because of the soft nature of the soil and the high annual precipitation. For very muddy conditions, however, knobblies can clog up and inhibit traction and overall cycling performance. For mountainous country that has many long descents, performance heavy-duty off-road tyres provide that extra grip and braking power. They are also ideal for sandy trails near the coast. Their multifaceted knobs and aggressive tread pattern give good cornering on loose surfaces but they lose efficiency if used on sealed roads. If the majority of cycling is to be on bitumen, changing to slicks can be well worthwhile. In addition to providing less rolling resistance, slicks can also increase grip around corners, permitting sharper banking angles. Some slicks contain an interwoven kevlar composite shield for puncture resistance. Try to buy tyres with a low hysteresis (measure of memory time) that can rebound quickly after being compressed or deformed. This results in longer life expectancy.

It's important to match tyre width sizes with rim sizes. If the tyre is too wide for the rim, the side load support will be compromised and this will translate to unstable cornering. Additionally, keep the tyres well-inflated to allow optimal handling and maintain momentum. The exceptions are on soft surfaces such as sand and mud, where the maximum surface area of the tyre profile is needed to maintain traction.

Following are three additional tyre accessories that off-road cyclists might like to consider to reduce the chances of a puncture:

- tyre liners that fit between the tube and the inside of the tyre
- rim tapes covering the sharp edges around the spoke holes
- extra thick thorn-proof tubes made from heavier rubber.

Some popular brand names are Tioga, Hutchinson, Michelin, IRC, Ritchie, Avocet and Panaracer. There is a lot of variation in compounds, side wall strength, tread patterns, kevlar linings and weight. Some tyres lend themselves well to downhill slopes, others to soft terrain or cornering, so it is a matter of selecting the right tyre to suit the predominant riding conditions. Your bike shop staff will know which tyre is suitable for the terrain you intend to ride in. Mountain biking magazines also have regular reviews and testing on each new major tyre released on the market.

Handlebar Attachments

Computers

Cycling computers have become dramatically cheaper and lighter over the last decade. Ever since the Cateye Velo CC-1000 set the standard for such features as digital readouts and average speed calculations, the trend has been to pack more features into a smaller unit. Indeed, today's computers are about half the size of their predecessors, built from lightweight plastics, and come in frame-matching colours for the fashion conscious. Standard models rarely cost more than $50 and are easy to fit.

Wheel circumferences can be entered into the computer, plus tyre sizes and the rider's weight. Regular functions include speed in kilometres or miles, trip

Recent technology: an Avolet Vertech altimeter watch and cycling computer.

Mt Wilson, Wollangambe wilderness, New South Wales.

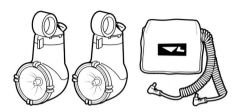

The Vistalite 400 series halogen lamp system.

distance and time, as well as an odometer, maximum speeds, a clock and calculation of average speeds. Battery life expectancy is normally two years. The accuracy is astounding and most computers can be easily detached when locking the bike up and leaving it in a public place. Another advantage is a motivational one: when you have a constant readout of your average speed, you are more likely to expend extra energy when climbing in order to maintain that figure.

When selecting a computer, ensure it is waterproof and that it functions even when the sensor is caked in mud. Some models can give one or more of three new additional information readouts, catering for hard-core enthusiasts:

● altimeter
● cadence readout and heart-rate monitor. By plugging additional sensors into the front crank and onto the rider's chest or wrist, a whole series of data about heart rate and performance can be generated over the duration of a ride.
● global positioning system: the ultimate in high-tech gadgets. By receiving data from a network of geostationary satellites around the Earth, an in-built computer can accurately calibrate one's longitude and latitude and also generate independent information of average speed, maximum speed and altitude. This type of computer is expensive and can cost anywhere up to $1000, even more for additional accessories that reconcile the data with topographical maps.

Lights

Cycling off-road at night can be dangerous. Lights can at times be more of a hindrance than a help because the travelling speed will be too slow for a dynamo to work effectively, so it might be safer to let your eyes adjust to the available light. One alternative is to use batteries but these are heavy and expensive. Halogen lamps are the most efficient, giving the brightest light for the least energy output. Also, being able to focus the beam at different lengths for different speeds and conditions can be useful. One of the best systems on the market is the Vistalite VL400 that uses a rechargeable, detachable ni-cad battery pack. The Vistalite has twin halogen lamps mounted on swivels that can be detached and used as a torch if required.

Bar-ends

These horn-like attachments can be more comfortable for ascending as they align more with the natural vertical position of the hand. Bar-ends are also used to ease strain on long rides, as they allow the rider an alternative hand grip position.

Frame attachments

Suspension forks

Despite initial concerns about the added weight and lower riding efficiency, shock absorbers have become one of the most spectacular areas of technological innovation. Front suspension forks have become virtually standard on all middle- and high-range bikes.

Along rough flat roads, kinetic energy expended perpendicular to the road surface is minimised with shock absorbers and forward momentum is maintained. In this respect, shock absorbers save energy that would normally be wasted in hitting a small obstacle such as a rock. Because the wheel moves up and over the obstacle, there is less resistance and therefore less energy used. Due to their adjustability and ever decreasing weight, even top-end riding professionals have them as standard equipment.

Reputable shock absorber brand names include Rock Shox, Manitou and Marzocchi. Look for shocks that are sloped forward, so that they start absorbing the shock before the wheel has passed over the obstacle.

Unlike front suspension that has a fairly standard design across the market, rear suspension configurations vary dramatically. Every manufacturer uses a different technique, trying on the one hand to maximise rigidity thereby reducing unwanted compression when pedalling, while on the other hand still maximising suspension travel when going downhill. Be wary of rear suspension designs that vary the distance between the front crank and the rear cluster during compression, as this can create problems with gear changes. A lot of suspension design research has been spent on correcting this problem, largely by making the bottom bracket the pivot point.

Bidon cages and bottles

Even though prices for water bottles vary between $5 and $40, all of them do much the same job. The fashion or weight conscious might prefer to invest in a fluoro-red bottle with a titanium cage but it will store the water no better than an inexpensive one purchased from the supermarket or department store.

Water bottles can be attached to the bike via bosses to any of the three major tubes of the frame or even to the handlebars. They can be detached and used as drink bottles when walking. Don't fill them with anything but water, as heat and time will make a mess of other solutions. Some have tyre-repair kits attached to them and others can be used as containers for snack food or a spare tube. Some bottles have a specially designed spill-free pull-top valve so they can be opened using only one hand.

The Adura/Apollo bidons have a 650 ml capacity (85 ml larger than normal) and have wide openings, enabling easier cleaning.

Clipless pedals and toe straps

The advent of clipless pedals has arisen out of competitive road and velodrome cycling. This type of pedal increases cycling efficiency because you can pull through the zero-torque point (when the pedals are in the 6 o'clock position) as well as push down. The other advantage is that they automatically position the ball of the foot over the centre of the pedal, the optimal riding position.

The innovations specific to mountain biking are in the area of recessed cleats in bike shoes. Because the cleat sits higher than the shoe's tread, cyclists can still walk normally when dismounted and mountain bike shoes have consequently developed into a semi-hiking shoe. Initially, there were different types of shoes on the market and one needed to buy the correct shoe to fit a certain pedal. But Shimano's SPD (Shimano Pedalling Dynamics) system has become the de-facto standard, developed specifically for the mountain bike market. The SPD pedals are often sold standard with more expensive bike models, and low—average price range purchasers will need to acquire the pedals separately.

The Shimano SH-M090 shoe and PD-M636 double-sided off-road racing pedals.

Some shoe manufacturers, such as Nike and Salomon, also sell specialised bike shoes. However, they are suited to one purpose and extended walking through mud, water and over boulders is not ideal. There is no substitute for a genuine hiking boot with proper tread and a waterproof lining.

There are several options in pedals, including the double-sided low-profile SPD-only pedals or downhill pedals that are surrounded by the traditional cage designed so that regular shoes can also be worn. Exiting out of the pedal is done by twisting the heel outwards or inwards. Release-tension and entry-position is fully adjustable and the pedal continues to work well in muddy conditions. For off-road cycling, an easy setting is necessary to ensure quick release when negotiating rough terrain. The novice rider may find the idea of being locked-in uncomfortable on very rough trails, but the experienced rider can find the system a bonus. The pedal will provide better control over the positioning of the rear wheel, making the bike more manoeuvrable over rocks, logs and other obstacles.

Like clipless pedals, toe straps can be a bit of a hassle to enter and exit. The disadvantage is that they have to be manually tightened to optimise efficiency.

Furthermore, they can prevent a quick escape during an accident. Despite these drawbacks, toe straps are popular on many mid-range mountain bikes.

Gel seats

One of the most common problems mountain cyclists experience is a tender backside from the constant shifting in the saddle. The Avocet Gelflex saddle, manufactured with spenco gel, distributes vertical and lateral pressure more evenly over the contact area and, unlike other gel saddles, it does not lose its elasticity in the colder temperatures a cyclist can experience at higher altitudes. Weight is kept to a minimum by varying the thickness of the gel in critical pressure points, and the nylon/lycra cover moves with the gel so that its hydrostatic properties are not diminished. There are various models on the market comprising various thicknesses and shapes, which cater for everyone from the casual weekend recreationalist to the professional competitor.

An Avocet Gelflex seat provides added comfort.

Other types of seats available include leather, air and split. The type of material used in the rails for attaching to the seat post to the bike is also varied and can dramatically affect the price. Chromoly (chrome-molybdenum), aluminium and titanium rails exist for mountain cyclists with lightweight bikes.

Lock

Depending on where you want to leave your bike, you may have to carry a lock. Some attractions in wilderness-based national parks can only be visited on foot. In this case, an infinite number of hiding places exist where the bike can be stashed for a few hours or a few days. Obviously locks are unnecessary here. However, if you are passing through a township and stop to stock up on food or equipment, or visit more popular tourist areas, it would be advisable to lock your bike.

A U-Lock or thick chain is most effective. One Australian example is the Rhode Gear Gorilla ATB lock, which is specifically designed for mountain bikes because it has a longer loop to fit wider tyres. It is made of high-tensile chromoly, has a ball bearing behind the lock to prevent drilling, and over 700,000 possible combinations.

Clothing

Pants

Two advantages of specialised cycling tights are that they absorb perspiration and offer some protection from grazing during a fall. However, you can enjoy the mountain biking experience perfectly well without them. Remember that the bush will lacerate cycling tights, especially if any rock-scrambling or bush-bashing is involved.

For colder months there now exists a range of thermal tights made of new high-tech water and wind-proof fabrics such as Activent and Gore-Tex.

Shirt

Special cycling shirts allow greater evaporation of perspiration but for the recreational mountain biker any T-shirt will do. Cotton is particularly unsuitable for cycling because it absorbs and retains water. For hot conditions, Macpac manufactures several types of Coolmax fabric shirts that allow perspiration to evaporate and block out the sun's UV rays.

Shoes

Normal sandshoes or sneakers are perfect footwear. If some lengthy or difficult walking is involved, a good pair of walking boots will be needed. If no walking is in store, shoes are the least important of all items for hopefully the feet will never touch the ground!

Special mountain bike shoes are now available which are made of materials such as carbon, nylon and glass fibre. According to the manufacturers, these shoes are supposed to be 'the most efficient tool ever designed for transferring energy from the foot to the drive chain'. While the stiff soles and recessed cleats of specialised mountain biking shoes are definitely an advantage when used in conjunction with SPD pedals (see page 28), walking can be dangerous because the metal cleat may be the only part of the shoe in contact with the ground. This means no grip on rocks when climbing and descending, and the constant slipping will rapidly wear down the metal to create entry and exit problems. In short, the wilder the terrain expected to be encountered the less useful clipless pedals and mountain biking shoes will be.

Gloves

Even in summer, cyclists in high-altitude alpine regions can experience below-freezing temperatures. Any gloves from home are adequate if cold weather and/or strong winds are expected. A pair of gloves might also be useful to prevent blisters or chaffing and to protect the hands from grazing during a fall. Special mountain biking gloves from Adura contain a 3 millimetre layer of neoprene for shock absorption. They cost about $35. The disadvantage is that during hot weather gloves can make the palms quite sweaty.

Glasses

If your eyes water when travelling at high speeds or in winds, or during hazy, glary days, cycling glasses definitely will make conditions more comfortable. Make sure they are shatterproof, scratch-resistant, reduce glare and block out all UV light. They'll also keep out insects. Some specialised mountain bike glasses come with a lycra band for retention and perspiration absorption. Like the glasses the Test cricketers wear, they are expensive: expect to pay anything up to $300. The disadvantage of wearing glasses is that bumps, holes and sand-patches in shadows on the trail will be more difficult to distinguish.

Descending steep inclines is best performed in a standing position with knees bent and leaning backwards.

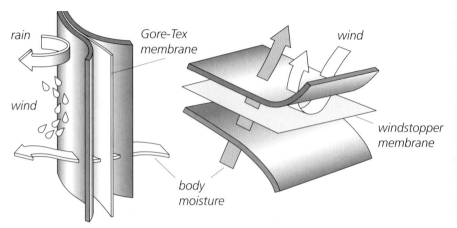

Gore-Tex.   Gore Windstopper fabric.

Waterproof jackets

Mountains attract violent weather changes because of their dynamic height variation and the nature of the topography can obscure storm fronts until they are almost overhead. These factors necessitate the wearing of an outer shell garment that is windproof, waterproof, breathable, lightweight and compactable.

The de-facto standard in worldwide adventuring is a jacket made from Gore-Tex material that satisfies all these requirements. This fabric is manufactured from a semipermeable, microporous membrane that allows the skin to breathe while preventing any external moisture from entering.

Mountain Designs carry a range of Gore-Tex jackets such as the Cirrostratus, which retails for about $300. The jacket is knee-length and contains a variety of pockets for maps, wallet and food.

For even harsher climates, Paddy Pallin sell the Vortex full-zip overpants to protect the legs from the elements. Made from Ripstop and three-layer Jura Gore-Tex, they sell for just over $350.

Windproof jackets

For colder alpine climates you will need a warmer jacket to go under the Gore-Tex shell. Fleece jackets such as Gore Windstopper or Polartec Windbloc are breathable, windproof, warm and moisture resistant and they sell for around $300.

Underwear

Moisture-wicking polypropylene or Polartec thermal underwear is the most effective insulation material that can be worn against the skin. These garments, available from Kathmandu, are extremely efficient in their warmth retention despite their compact size and low weight. They cost about $100 for a set of top and bottom.

Thermal clothes

For extreme conditions you will need a set of thermal insulation, waterproof gloves and socks. Sealskinz socks are insulated by Thermax and contain a waterproofing membrane from Du-Pont that is perfect for high-rainfall muddy areas such as south-west Tasmania and Fiordland in New Zealand's South Island.

When dressing for warmth, a three-layer approach is both optimal and flexible. The first layer is thermal underwear that keeps the skin dry, then a breathable fleece layer for maximum warmth retention and finally an outer Gore-Tex waterproof shell to keep out wind and rain.

Other touring equipment

Day pack

When venturing out into the wilderness, the mountain biker's main luggage carrier will be a day pack, preferably one that is divided up into three or more compartments. It should be comfortable, have a waist strap and enough room for plenty of water, food, maps and a camera.

Macpac stock an excellent range of small packs such as the 35 litre Ultra-marathon. Besides having a comfortable and comprehensive harness, it also can fit the optional Macpac Oasis water bladder. This is a 3.2 litre collapsible carrier which can be inserted into a special sleeve in the day pack. A hose then attaches onto the shoulder strap so you can drink at all times without having to take the pack off. The complete system sells for about $220.

Altimeter

For the statistically minded, a wristwatch altimeter like the Avocet Vertech can give some interesting information. The in-built barometer converts air pressure into accurate altitude readouts. Even when ascending small hills, the readout updates altitude changes every second. Furthermore, the barometer records accumulated height gained over a longer trip and can even be useful for predicting weather. For example, if you have set up camp and the readout indicates air pressure is falling, a front may be approaching. The Avocet Vertech automatically compensates for temperature differentials and wind does not affect its accuracy, which can aid in navigational queries.

Water bladders

Also known as 'camel backs' or 'hydration packs', these popular accessories address the need for mountain bikers to constantly rehydrate themselves. They come in various sizes and have the advantage of being lightweight and easy to use. One example is the 6 litre One Planet H_2O pack, which can be used on its own or attached onto other One Planet backpacks. A hose from the clear plastic bladder in the pack can be attached on the front harness so that you can drink as you ride. One word of warning: don't use powdered flavours in the water on hot days unless the bladder is flushed out immediately, as bacteria can accumulate in the bladder from the sugar residue. They will last longer if they are filled only with clear, purified water. Keep the bladder refrigerated before each ride.

The Lowepro Photo Trekker AW.

Special-use packs

There are special packs available for carrying gear such as photographic equipment. Expensive cameras would only get damaged in panniers with the constant vibration. Lowepro makes a series of specific photographic backpacks, such as the Photo Trekker AW, which comes with its own protective waterproof material in case of rain. The Photo Trekker can house 35 mm SLR and medium-format cameras, with separate compartments for lenses, filters, film and other accessories.

Blue waterholes in northern Kosciuszko National Park, New South Wales.

On day trips, a regular 20-30 litre day pack may not be large enough to carry a change of warm weather gear and other necessities. That's why a medium-sized pack, like the Macpac Rocketeer or One Planet Mistress can be very handy. They're just as strong as a full, heavy-duty overnight pack but without the additional weight. They can hold around 40–50 litres in several versatile compartments.

Camping

After some preliminary day rides around the local area or in the nearest national park, overnight camping is usually the next step undertaken. The times immediately before, during and after sunset really give nature an ambience that day visitors miss out on.

As with day-trip equipment, purchase only essential gear for the first camping trip and update your inventory once experience and ambition take hold. Be prepared to spend $1000–2000 on overnight gear as the difference in quality between specialist equipment from reputable outdoor stores and supermarket brands is substantial. Good sleeping bags, packs and tents will last for decades but, more importantly, your life may one day depend on your investment.

Sleeping Bag

These range enormously in price. Supermarkets sell cheap bags at around $40 for synthetic polyester models that weigh 2–3 kilograms. These bags are adequate for all summer camping in relatively warm coastal climates. Slightly up-market are synthetic Quallofill bags that keep relatively warm even when wet. The disadvantage is that they are very bulky.

It is difficult, however, to go past a fill that is comprised mainly of duck or goose down. Coming mostly from China, down is by far the best insulator because of its air-trapping qualities. Furthermore, down bags are light (1–2 kilograms) and can compress to incredibly small sizes. The damage? From $250 to $900 depending on the amount and ratio of the fill. The upmarket models have waterproof Gore-Tex exteriors but unless you are planning to cycle in Antarctica or camp underwater, they are not necessary.

The Mountain Designs stores have a complete range of down sleeping bags, some of which are treated with a dry-loft water-resistant and windproof exterior. Their compactability makes them perfect for mountain cyclists with

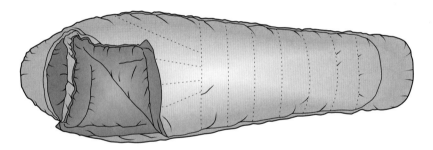

Mummy-style sleeping bag.

Adventure One's Earth Mat.

volume and weight constraints. A model that has excellent warmth for most four-season conditions, is lightweight and compresses into a small volume is the Mountain Designs Standhart, selling for around $600.

Accessories available for sleeping bags include large storage bags, as down should not be compressed when not in use, and silk and cotton inner sheets for extra warmth. Pally Pallin stores sell a full Gore-Tex bivvy outer lining that completely waterproofs the sleeping bag, reducing the need for a tent. Although it costs $500, it compacts to a minute size and weighs less than a kilogram, which your back muscles will appreciate for many years to come.

Sleeping mat

Foam, closed-cell sleeping rolls are unbeatable for their price. Supermarkets sell them for about $20, although some can cost up to $65. When camping in cold or damp conditions, be aware that the ground will drain heat away during the night because the sleeping bag filler underneath you will be compressed. Proper insulation can be provided only with self-inflating foam mattresses that are smaller than their closed-cell counterparts, but cost anything between $90 and $200. They provide a cushion of air that shields the body from the ground. The main disadvantage (besides their cost) is that they can puncture. There are various brands now on the market, but the Therma-A-Rest models from Cascade Designs have the strongest reputation. Their mattresses vary in length, material, thickness and price. Among the most popular is the Staytek Lite Long. Weighing just 850 grams, it contains die-cut foam encased in a waterproof nylon taffeta. The top surface is comprised of a specially woven fabric that prevents slippage while the bottom is a fast-drying nylon that resists dirt and dampness. It is an ideal compromise between insulation and weight, costing about $160. To go with this mat, you can also purchase a repair kit and stuff sack. In addition, Cascade Designs manufacture polyester fibre-filled pillows that compress quite tightly and allow additional clothing to be inserted for extra bulk. All are available from stores such as Mountain Designs. Adventure One manufactures a lightweight Earth Mat in a mummy-like shape that approximates the human contour and so minimises bulk.

Backpack

Depending on the type of expedition being planned, a backpack may be prefer-able to a set of panniers. Backpacks can be more comfortable and flexible if you

One Planet's 'mistress' pack.

want to camp away from the formed trails, leaving the bike behind. There are dozens of quality brands available. When choosing which one to buy, make sure the harness is fully adjustable so that weight is distributed evenly between the shoulders and hips. Although external compartment packs are rare these days, most good packs have several internal compartments for dividing up gear.

The pack should be waterproof and accommodate enough equipment for at least a week's ride. Such a model is the popular 70 litre Mountain Designs Federation Peak, which uses a very clever fully customisable harness system to maximise comfort without being unnecessarily heavy. It is equipped with external straps for sleeping mats and tents as well as having outside compartments for easy access to items needed throughout the day, such as maps and snacks. Be prepared to spend above $400 for such a robust pack, but it will last many a tough trek.

If you are travelling overseas and want a hybrid between a backpack and a suitcase, the Kashgar Travel Pack from Kathmandu offers the perfect compromise. One Planet also manufactures an overnight pack (the Bass) in 65 litre and 75 litre models that has a detachable 26 litre day pack for the ultimate in flexibility.

Tent

When camping on clear summer nights by the coast, a simple fly will do perfectly to keep off the dew. When you are venturing into uncertain territory, however, where sudden weather changes are unpredictable, a sealed tent is highly recommended.

Price depends on the material, design, brand name and size. If you are cycling in a group, the weight of the tent can be shared. The application of a seam sealant and the use of a group sheet, preferably a space blanket, can improve water resistance.

Eureka manufactures several popular tent models. Styles and sizes range from one-person bivvy-style tents to models made for use in snow expeditions.

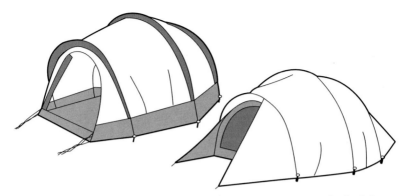

A Eureka Polar Storm tent without the fly (left) and with the fly (right).

The Bike and Hike design weighs under 2 kilograms, has a floor area of about 3.5 square metres, a frame of shock-corded 7000 series aircraft aluminium that compacts to a size small enough to fit easily into any backpack, and a design that reduces buffeting if pitched with its longitudinal axis aligned with prevailing winds. The cost is approximately $300. This tent is fast to erect, sleeps two comfortably and comes with a fly that can be zipped open on mild nights. Two entrances ensures cross-ventilation. Eureka's other cycling/walking models include the Moonshadow and the one-person Gossamer. For cyclists venturing into rugged, high-altitude terrain on extended excursions, the Caddis offers superb four-season protection with ease of erection. It is a comfortable 180 centimetres wide with two vestibules and it can be pitched with or without the fly. The tent weighs 3.5 kilograms and costs about $600.

Recent tent designs have taken advantage of new lightweight materials and technology. The classic new-age tent is the self-supporting dome. Gone are the days of carrying heavy steel frames, canvas tenting, plastic ground floors, pegs and ropes. The self-supporting dome tent is lightweight, has excellent space-to-weight ratio, good headroom, stability, ease and speed of erection, can be pitched on rock and, once set up, can be picked up and placed elsewhere. The only disadvantage with self-supporting tents is that they can be blown away when unoccupied, so always throw in all the sleeping gear immediately after setting up. The two-person Apollo from Macpac's Horizon series is self-supporting, although the fly needs two pegs to secure it. This tent sells for about $500 and is available in all good camping stores.

Approaching Round Mountain in the Snowys, New South Wales.

The tunnel-style tent (sometimes crossbred with the dome, forming what is called a 'dunnel') is also popular. Incorporating vestibules (an area between the tent wall and the fly), they are very light and suitable for exposed, high-altitude conditions. These are what the professional mountaineers use and some models cost as much as $1300.

Ground sheet

The common space blanket can be bought at disposal stores everywhere and is by far the most popular groundsheet. Uses include:

- a floor when using a fly so sleeping bags don't get dirty
- an extra tent floor to help prevent heat escaping and water leaking in
- a picnic 'rug' for meals to spread out cooking utensils and food
- an emergency blanket for victims of hypothermia and heat exhaustion.

With the silver side out, the blanket will reflect some 70 per cent of external radiation and keep the body cool. The dark side is placed outside in the event of hypothermia so all external radiation is absorbed and internal radiation is reflected back.

Pack towels

A pack towel is a very useful multipurpose 68 x 25 centimetre cloth made from 100 per cent viscose that can hold up to 10 times its weight in water. This water can be 92 per cent rung out by hand and the remainder quickly dries when exposed to air. Weighing just 42 grams, it is the ideal towel for the mountain biker. Use it to dry the skin, as insulation for handling hot pots, for cleaning the dishes, as a neckerchief for sweat absorption or as a medical compress.

Gear checklist

The following is a suggested checklist of equipment that you may need when camping overnight. It is by no means comprehensive, and you may want to add or delete items according to preference. It is wise to draw up such a list so nothing is forgotten at the last minute. What could be worse than realising after a long day's ride that there's no can-opener?

Despite the long list, the equipment should not weigh more than 12–15 kilograms. Add another kilogram of food per day and you are looking at about 20 kilograms of luggage for a week's trip. This would be the maximum weight for any cyclist to carry.

COOKING	HYGIENE	MISCELLANEOUS
billy	toothbrush and paste	lighter/matches
frying pan	soap (natural)	candle
pots/saucepan	toilet paper	maps
plate	trowel	water bottle
cup	water	pocket-knife
cutlery	first-aid kit	sleeping bag
fuel stove and fuel	tissues	sleeping mat
can-opener	insect repellent	tent and/or fly
scouring pad	sun block	pillow sack
	comb	MTB repair kit
	deodorant	spare tube
		torch
		clothing

Photography

Mountain biking can take you into the most spectacular country. Capturing the scenery on film can be rewarding, one made possible by the additional carrying capacity of a mountain bike. If photography is your interest, Robert Rankin's *Wilderness Light*, is an excellent non-technical book that discusses composition, subject and lighting aspects of photography in national parks.

Camera

A 35 mm camera with manual settings is recommended so that you can compensate for measuring inaccuracies of the light meter. Fog, high contrast, direct sunlight, position of subject and long shadows can all lead to incorrect exposure evaluations. Furthermore, a manual mode will give you more control when photographing waterfalls and other time-exposure shots. Those photographers with commercial aspirations may consider upgrading to medium format (for example, 6 x 7) to provide maximum magazine-quality definition in your photographs.

Lenses

Ideally, a standard lens, a macro and a telephoto will give optimal results since the number of glass elements in the lens is kept to a minimum, allowing maximum resolution. Generally, the lower the f-stop (for example, f1.8), the better quality the lens. Despite having a higher f-stop, a good zoom lens will do the job of many lenses and still give more than adequate definition. Many of the photographs in this book were taken with a 28–200mm (f3.5 to f22) lens.

Film

Although the quality gap between print and transparency film is narrowing, transparenices still produce the best results in terms of colour saturation and resolution. The use of a low-ASA rated film can most faithfully reproduce nature's colours. An award-winning high resolution17-layer emulsion film from Fuji called Velvia 50ASA enhances greens superbly in both direct and indirect light as well as giving very fine detail. The disadvantages with slide films is that they're usually more expensive, the results are more difficult to view and there is limited scope for corrections during processing. Exposures have to be spot on, whereas with negative film, one can make alterations of up to two stops.

Tripod

In addition to a camera, you will need a tripod. Rainforest canopies, narrow valleys, flowing river shots and waterfalls all require time exposures of anything up to 30 seconds. The tripod should be lightweight and compactable. There are numerous models that cater directly for the outdoor trekker. Tripods will also permit the solo cyclist to take self-portraits. On occasion, a forked tree or well-positioned boulder can prove a handy substitute for a tripod.

Filters

Polarising filters are usually unnecessary as they reduce the amount of light entering the camera by up to two stops and they become less useful when there is diffused light. Windy, fresh conditions ensure a minimum of haze over landscapes so most of the time a skylight (UV) filter is also unnecessary. Some forest vistas can become extremely hazy on hot calm days. Consequently, a polarising filter will help to make features more defined.

Tips

Good results are the product of three factors: equipment, environment and skill. The following tips will help you produce the best results:

- For most types of photography, direct sunlight will give better colour and contrast than overcast conditions.
- Early morning and evening are the best times to photograph. This is because the lower angle of the sun's rays through the atmosphere removes blue light, giving a warmer shift.
- Prevailing misty conditions are good for mood shots: calm lakes, trunks of beech trees, dew droplets on spider webs and moss.
- Avoid using a flash because it washes out colours. Cave formations are best captured using a tripod and a long exposure using the installed coloured lights. Back-lit shawls especially come out well using this technique.
- For landscapes, include a foreground where possible, such as a person, boulder or shrub. This gives the picture depth of field, highlighting distance.
- When using a polarising filter, photograph as much 'with' the sun as possible, although good polarising effects also occur when shooting at 90 degrees to the sun.
- Avoid having the horizon passing through the middle of the frame. Make a habit of angling the camera slightly down, so the horizon is only a short

distance from the top of the frame. The only exceptions would be in unusual cases where cloud formations are particularly dramatic.

● For shots of cyclists at lookouts, choose a smaller aperture (f18 if possible); good polarising effects also occur when taken 90 degrees to the sun.

● The top of the frame. The only exceptions would be in unusual cases where cloud formations are as still as possible.

● Rivers, seascapes, cascades and waterfalls can have the classic softened effect by slowing the exposure to as much as 10 seconds. However, too long an exposure will start to produce a blue shift without the suitable correction filter.

Not all that looks good to the eye will look good on film. Only experience will improve one's judgement of what will make a good photograph. Comparing results to records of exposure settings will also improve the accuracy of compensation adjustments so that a smaller percentage of film is wasted.

Clearing a puddle.

RIDING A MOUNTAIN BIKE

4

This chapter contains a few handy tips that will improve your cycling ability, efficiency and safety, and make cycling a more enjoyable activity. It is always best to learn the right way the first time, so that very quickly your new skills will become a matter of habit.

The single most important part of cycling is fitness. The fit cyclist on the beaten-up single-geared BMX will *always* beat the unfit cyclist on the $20,000 custom titanium 30-speed dual-suspension bike.

After purchasing the right bike and adjusting the handlebars and seat height for comfort, the urge to try it out will be irrepressible. People converting to mountain bikes from touring or racing bikes will immediately notice that greater effort is necessary to achieve high speeds. The reason is in the thicker tyres and in the more upright seating position. The higher gears will also be lower ratios, while gear levers will be positioned on top of the straight handlebars. Those accustomed to lifting their bike up stairs will also find a few extra kilograms of metal separate a mountain bike from a touring bike.

Cycling in our rugged mountains is different from all other forms of cycling. Concentration is directed away from maintaining 'rhythm' to focusing on avoiding obstacles. The mountain biker has to constantly make choices in steering, braking, balance and gearing. These skills will develop through the negotiation of rough, winding fire trails, ducking overhanging branches, crossing streams and descending narrow cliff passes.

Novice cyclists can acquire these riding skills by enrolling in one of many various mountain biking courses or organised tours available.

Climbing

There are three methods of climbing: walking, spinning and honking.

Walking (also known as first gear)

Many hills cannot be conquered on a bike, no matter how many cogs the clusters have. But even pushing a bike uphill can be faster than normal walking because the upper body can be rested on the handlebars. Experiment with different techniques: push in short bursts with rests, or in one slower, consistent uphill trudge. The break-even point where cycling has no energy efficiency advantage over walking is about a 20° incline. Any steeper and walking is more energy efficient.

Spinning

Choose a very low gear and stay seated the entire length of the slope. The seat has to be positioned quite high. Concentrate on maintaining cadence (the number of pedal rotations per minute). If the rear wheel starts to spin in the dirt or mud, get up and lean back to put more pressure on it to increase traction. Although walking seems like the easier alternative, cycling up a gradual slope actually requires *less* effort but is more tiring because the muscles are required to emit much more energy per unit of time. This is the preferred method for professional competitors.

Honking

This method is used for steeper, shorter slopes and a higher gear is selected while standing up and leaning forward. But perhaps the most efficient way is a combination of honking and spinning because the variation temporarily relieves certain muscles. However, there is no substitute for a good level of fitness.

While climbing, a water bottle is almost essential for cooling down. Expending just 74 watts of energy, a cyclist can maintain an average speed of 22 km/h on level ground and the 22 km/h headwind will ensure adequate heat dissipation. But on a 1:6 slope, only 2.4 km/h can be maintained at the same 74-watt power output, resulting in at least double the energy used to remain stable. However, heat dissipation without a regular drink will prevent this level of output from being maintained.

Positions for climbing and descending.

When climbing, weight over the rear wheel has to be maintained to maximise traction.

Attitude is also important. Think positively about the hill: it will be another obstacle out of the way, the destination will be closer, there will be a good view at the top and, best of all, there will be a downhill on the other side.

Descending

As always in life, the fun things are the most dangerous. Physics defines force as proportional to the square of the bicycle's velocity. This implies that there will be a point where braking resistance is insufficient in stopping a fully laden bike on a steep slope if the rider allows it to accelerate too much. Always try to use constant pressure on the rear brake *alone* to slow down. If it is not enough, lean back to put more pressure on the rear tyre. If the bike is still accelerating, gradually apply the front brake. Never speed up and then suddenly squeeze the brakes at the last minute; you might fall further than you expect—six feet further!

When at the top of a steep, long descent, stop and quickly check the brakes and anything else that might be loose. Most cyclists hate having to stop halfway through a terrific descent.

Brake with the rear brake first when descending.

Obstacles

Imagine flying down a fantastic trail, the trees a blur, your adrenalin surging. Suddenly, turning a corner, a fallen tree lies across the track. There's not enough time to brake, so your only alternative is to pass over the log. How? By jumping.

Begin a jump by waiting until your strongest leg is on top. Then suddenly lean back on the handlebars, lifting the front wheel off the ground, while simultaneously pushing down the pedal. With some practice a 'wheelie' can be maintained for about 2–3 seconds. When you have mastered this, lift the front wheel again while standing on the pedals and raise both legs, at the same time throwing your body weight forward. This motion, called a bunny-hop, should lift the rear wheel off the ground. By coordinating the wheelie with the bunny-hop, with practice you should be able to clear small objects. Don't worry too much if the rear wheel doesn't actually become airborne, because the reduced pressure off the ground will be sufficient to tackle the majority of obstacles. Bunny-hopping, of course, cannot be done with a bike that has excessive luggage attached. Descents under those conditions must, therefore, be more controlled.

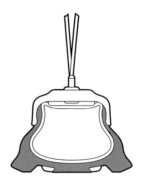

Cross-section of a tyre and inner-tube (top). Decreasing the inner tube pressure (bottom) can increase the surface area of the tyres for conditions where traction is crucial.

Rocks and ledges

The technique when negotiating descents down platforms, ledges and large rocks is quite simple: *lean back!* This has two effects. First, it stops the bike from flipping over when

Pioneering mountain biking venue in the Mersey River Valley, Tasmania.

the front wheel drops down to the next level, and second, it increases the braking power of the rear wheel.

Falling

Instinct dictates to release one hand to protect you from a fall but statistics reveal that doing so often leads to a sprained or broken wrist. Experts advise to keep your hands on the bars, thus protecting the arms. Difficult to practise this one! Wearing cycling gloves can help prevent grazing.

Cornering

Avoid excessive leaning in on turns when the ground is loose. Rather, take the corner slowly and drift from inside to outside.

Sand and mud

When approaching a sandy patch, accelerate and coast straight over it. Avoid steering, gear and acceleration changes when in the sand as they can all result in a loss of momentum. If a lot of sand is to be expected on your ride, deflate the tyres by about 10 psi. The best conditions for traversing sand occur during or just after rain. Wet sand is much easier to ride across—the same principle applies when choosing the best section on the beach to jog or cycle on. Similar techniques apply to negotiating mud. Don't worry too much about getting mud off during a ride. Most of it will come off by itself. Avoid skidding in soft wet ground as erosion is greatly accelerated. These bogs are just as likely to occur on plateau tops as by rivers.

Fording

Always make sure there are no large river rocks in the ford when you are crossing streams. Don't ride too slowly because loss of momentum could be embarrassing in a strong current. Also, watch out for exposed concrete mesh

Negotiating rocky terrain in the Blue Mountains, New South Wales.

on fords. When riding in a group, cross large streams one at a time in single file. If the stream is a strong one from overnight rain and debris is being washed down, it is better to walk the bike across. As a rule of thumb, any fast-flowing water above 40 centimetres deep, especially if the bottom is uncertain, may be unsafe to ride across.

Headwinds

When cycling in open country, nothing can be more frustrating than a headwind. It doesn't matter if you have the latest high-tech lightweight bike and have trained for years—a headwind can make you feel like a first-timer on a steel BMX with rusted hubs. Murphy's Law of cycling dictates that there will always be a headwind, no matter which direction, how fast or what time of day. Fortunately, mountain bikers spend a lot of their time under tree cover and so are sheltered from most incessant headwinds.

General

Always watch out for traffic coming the other way. Blind corners, especially when descending fast, are just as dangerous for cyclists as for motorists. Be aware that the trail could be open to four-wheel drivers, walkers, cyclists and equestrians coming the other way.

When unsure about a stream-bed, it's better to walk through.

MAINTENANCE AND REPAIRS

5

A new bike fresh from the shop is always going to function well, even if it's a supermarket no-frills model with cheap componentry. However, after the cables stretch, the brakes loosen, the gear-springs weaken and the spokes re-tension, the bike will never be exactly the same. This is why maintenance is such an essential ingredient to cycling. Even top-of-the-range Shimano XTR componentry will eventually fail if not looked after.

Maintenance is not about keeping the bike in new condition. It's about slowing the rate of equipment failure. Despite what many sales staff, cyclists, owners' handbooks and maintenance guides say, it's impossible to restore a bike to its shop condition after a few rides. Perhaps sometime in the future, manufacturers will design bikes that don't need cables or spokes or pad-based brakes. One can only hope.

Whether it's pumping up the tyres or reconstructing the rear wheel, some technical knowledge will be called for. There are many good books available that cover this subject, the definitive being Van der Plas' *Mountain Bike Maintenance*. However, books like this can quickly become useless because of the rapidly changing technology and the wide range of systems and group-sets on the market. Shimano alone has over a dozen componentry sets on the market. The best way to look after your bike, therefore, is to follow the advice contained in the maintenance manuals that accompany the bike when purchased. It is important that cyclists should endeavour to learn these maintenance skills rather than simply letting bike shops maintain the bikes on their behalf. This ensures self-sufficiency when out in the wilderness.

Before each ride

A bike store will overhaul your bike for you but it is preferable that you do this type of regular maintenance at home in order to become familiarised with the componentry. Before embarking on any mountain bike excursion, quickly carry out the following four-point check:

1 *Tyres* Ensure the tube is fully inflated: usually around 50–70 psi (276–344 kilopascals). For slicks, this can be as high as 85 psi (586 kilopascals).
2 *Brakes* The bike should be impossible to move forwards or backwards when both brakes are applied. Remember, when travelling over 30 km/h, 10 metres are needed to stop. On dirt roads or steep downhills, or in wet weather, minimum braking distances are significantly increased. Adjust brakes if necessary.
3 *Chain* Lubricate if dry.
4 *Wheels* Tighten if there is any lateral movement in the rims.

If you are planning a major ride of several days' duration, it would be wise to overhaul the bike:

1 Regrease all bearings. A lithium-based grease will provide good protection. Do not use oil.
2 Lubricate all cables and moving parts, such as the flywheel and derailleur pivot points, with a graphite-in-solution lubricant. Specific MTB oils, such as Finish Line, are based on teflon, trilinium and paraffin which not only reduces friction but gives rust protection, improves water resistance and does not attract grime.
3 Check for even spoke tension.
4 Check for wear in the chain wheels and shifting mechanism.
5 Tighten all nuts and bolts.
6 Replace brake blocks if worn.

Repairs on the trail

Identifying mechanical errors can begin with associating the sound with one of two areas: the pedals or the wheels. If a particular sound occurs only when pedalling, it could be the chain or the crankcase. If the sound coincides with the wheels turning, then suspect the rims hitting the brakes or a loose spoke.

Some of the shock of uneven terrain can be absorbed by standing up, with the knees slightly bent.

Punctures

Locate small holes by filling the tube with air and immersing it in water. If there is no water available, rotate the inflated tube next to your ear and listen for the hiss of escaping air. When you have located the hole, clean the area around it and rub with sandpaper to ensure adhesiveness of the patch. Apply the patch and press hard and flat, ensuring there are no raised edges. Wait 5–10 minutes to dry before inserting the tube back into the tyre.

Always take a spare tube with you in case the puncture is too big for a patch or is too close to the valve. As a last resort, grass and bracken ferns can be stuffed inside the tyre. They must be replaced every few kilometres because heat and friction quickly displace any moisture in the plant and all that is left is brown dust. Shift your weight off the wheel as you ride.

If the tyre is slashed, cutting a small square off a foam sleeping mat and pressing it between the inner tyre wall and the tube will usually alleviate the problem until the nearest bike store is reached.

Punctures are best repaired at home under controlled conditions. Once the hole is found the tube needs to be cleaned of dirt and, after patching, it is necessary to wait 5–10 minutes for the glue to set properly. That's why carrying a spare tube is the most convenient remedy.

1 Tools required to repair a puncture.

2 Unhooking the brakes.

4 Removing the wheel.

6 Using tyre levers to remove the tyre.

Follow these steps to repair a tyre:

1   When the inevitable bang and hiss occurs, find some flat ground. Don't continue a downhill run as the rim could become buckled. Lay the tools out on the ground together so individual items can't get lost.

2   Unhook the brakes by squeezing the brake arms together at the top where the most leverage can be obtained. There should be enough slack in the cable to get the fastening noodle out of its slot.

3   Remove any computer unit or light off the handlebar and turn the bike upside down.

4   Remove the wheel. Undo the quick-release skewer on the hub and wind the knob on the other side a few turns to loosen it. The wheel should just slide off.

5   Inspect the outside of the tyre for thorns or tears in the sidewall.

6   Remove the tyre from the rim. Plastic tyre levers with a tapered end on one side and a grooved hook on the other are the most effective way of removing the rubber. They're found in most good puncture repair kits. Lift one sidewall out and secure it to the spoke with the hooked end. Once the other lever is inserted, it will be quite easy to run it all the way around the rim. Only one edge of the tyre needs to be removed.

7   Remove the punctured tube by reaching under the tyre and pulling the tube out. This is best begun from the valve.

8   Inspect the rim and tyre. Look underneath and also feel the inside of the tyre to check there is no penetration of any sharp

objects. Also make sure the rim liner is covering the spoke holes.

9   Locate the puncture. This may be difficult if it's only a pinprick. The most reliable method is to inflate the tube and listen for hissing. If it's a very slow leak, submersing will release bubbles, identifying the puncture. Once the puncture is located, mark it with some chalk. If you are carrying a spare tube, proceed to Step 11.

7   Removing the tube.

10 Repair the puncture. Clean the area around the puncture to remove all dirt and dust and rough it up with some sandpaper so that the glue will stick. Peel off the patch from its backing and apply the glue liberally, ensuring the edges are covered. Also apply some glue to the area around the hole on the tube. Then firmly press the patch to the tube. Maintain this pressure for about 10 minutes, making sure the edges are flush.

8   Inspecting the tube.

11 Install the repaired or spare tube. From the same side of the tyre that the tube was first removed, slip the tube in, once again starting with the valve. It's always a good idea to slightly inflate the tube first to make sure there is no pinching.

11 Replacing the tube.

12 Place the tyre sidewall back in the rim. Strong fingers are needed to put the tyre in its place, although once again the tyre levers can help with lifting the final tight section into place.

13 Inflate the tube slowly, keeping an eye on the tyre and ensuring it's expanding evenly and no part of the tube is protruding or pinched between the rim and the tyre wall.

12 Replacing the tyre.

13 Inflating the tyre, ensuring no pinching.

14   Re-install the wheel and brakes. Confirm that the direction of the tyre tread conforms to the specifications written on the tyre wall. Tread patterns are manufactured to maximise grip when rotating in a specific direction. Take all garbage home, including the adhesive patch-backings.

Both Specialised and Hutchinson have produced tubes that contain a built-in sealant that self-repairs small punctures.

Squeaking brakes
This is probably due to a dirty or wet rim or, at worst, worn pads. Fortunately, these are one of the cheapest mountain-biking consumables to replace.

Weak brakes
Worry. At best, it is just a wet rim or some oil that has dripped down from the cluster. Wiping the rim and block and braking hard a number of times will remove the problem. At worst, it could be due to bent braze-ons. If it's the rear brake, you could probably continue riding until the next bike store. But *never* ride in the mountains without a properly functioning front brake.

Slipping chain
This occurs when the rear derailleur is out of adjustment, usually because the bike was leaning against a tree with the gear assembly pressing against the trunk. Simply adjusting the 'high' and 'low' screws in the adjustment mechanism with a Phillips head screwdriver will bring the chain back into line with the gears. At worst, the slipping could be due to a worn chain or even a worn rear cluster cog. These would need replacing. Remain in low gear until civilisation is reached and avoid riding up hills.

Steering out of alignment
Either the bike has been seriously abused or the headset bearings are loose. These can be tightened by means of a large shifter. New headset technology from the major manufacturers considerably reduces the likelihood of this happening.

Broken spoke

Things are starting to get serious. Replacing a broken spoke, especially in the rear wheel, is about the equivalent of a human bypass operation. Specialised tools are needed for most bikes, and even with these the operation takes about half an hour. The entire hub assembly has to be taken out piece by piece, including the bearings. The new spoke is then inserted and tightened. Then the wheel needs readjusting so it spins without wobble.

The bandaid solution is to simply twist off the broken spoke, take as much weight off the wheel as possible by moving luggage forward or backward or giving it to another cyclist and then coast to the nearest bike store.

But spokes in the rear wheel might soon be outdated with the recent development of carbon/kevlar wheels that give greater suspension, durability, energy efficiency and less wind resistance. The Tioga Disc Drive is manufactured from thermoplastic, alloy mesh and kevlar cord arranged in a geodesic pattern of angular and tangential cords to form a continuous tensioned linkage between hub and rim. They are unsuitable for the front wheel, however, because of the possibility of a strong crosswind making steering difficult. Some spokeless wheels have blades that actually produce lift in a crosswind!

Bent links

Twisted links in the chain are not a serious problem. A small chain-breaker or chain-removing tool and some spare links will rectify the problem easily. Simply remove the bent links with the chain-removing tool and replace them with an equal number of spare links. The entire operation normally takes about 10 minutes. Be careful not to lose the tiny crucial link-pins as these can be very fiddly to re-insert. Apply some lubricant to the new links so they glide around the cog wheels easily.

Uneven pedalling

A loose crankcase is usually the cause of this problem. It can be easily tightened with a shifter. If it happened just after an accident, suspect a bent chainwheel or pedal axle.

Broken rack stay

Normally caused by people overloading their panniers and riding as fast as possible over branches, rocks and ledges. Usually only one of the stays would

Kanangra Walls, Blue Mountains, New South Wales.

have been broken. This one can be fastened up to the bottom of the seat by some strong string. Transfer as much weight as possible from that pannier to the other end of the bike, a backpack or a fellow cyclist. This remedy will also solve a broken seat-post attachment, usually the weakest link between the rack and the frame.

After each ride

Whether the bike has spent an hour or a month on the dirt, it will be dirty, either from dust or mud. Usually both. Hose it down straight away and spray all moving parts with some form of WD spray to protect against rust. This is doubly important for cyclists living near the coast. Don't believe the people who say its cool to have your bike covered in grime.

Major services

An annual service with an authorised dealer will ensure that everything is tightened, greased and oiled. They should also be able to touch-up scratched paintwork. Many components, such as derailleurs, clusters, rapidfire gears and the crankcase, require the use of specialised tools such as torque meters.

FIRST AID, FITNESS AND NUTRITION

First aid

The most likely cause of injury faced by the cyclist is a fall. A simple medical kit with disinfectant and bandages is adequate for most types of grazing. For minor scrapes, bumps and small grazes it will be perfectly all right to continue on your ride.

However, with any major loss of blood there will be a loss of stamina, plus there is also the risk of shock and infection. At this point the planned route will have to be altered to the easiest and quickest way back to civilisation. Infection can also be caused by serious cases of saddle soreness where the combination of chaffing and perspiration cause cracks in the skin where bacteria can enter.

First-aid kits can be obtained from camping stores, the Red Cross and chemists. Homemade medical kits of individual items purchased from a pharmacy or supermarket are the cheaper and sometimes better approach. For cycling, the following components are recommended:

- sterilised bandages (about 15 metres)
- large gauze dressings (non-adhesive)
- small scissors
- disinfectant/antiseptic powder
- cottonwool
- plaster adhesive tape
- aspirin or paracetamol tablets.

Having regular breaks reduces fatigue and minimises the risk of accidents.

Grazing

The aim of treatment is to minimise loss of blood and the risk of infection. Clean the wound with water to remove any dirt caught in the open area. Cover the graze with antiseptic powder or tea tree oil, then apply a large gauze dressing and bandage. Treat for shock by giving warm liquids and allow some time to rest. If it is late in the day—and statistics confirm that risk of accident increases dramatically with time spent cycling—start looking for a campsite nearby so the injured cyclist can rest overnight.

Blisters

The repetition of pedalling in ill-fitting shoes can cause blisters, especially around the heel area. Apply an adhesive foam patch such as a bandaid and wear extra socks. If possible do not break the blister until returning home, as open wounds increase the risk of infection.

Snakebite

The accepted procedure for snakebite is surprisingly simple to learn:

1 Apply pressure on the wound.
2 At the same time, starting from the top of the limb (shoulder or thigh), bandage tightly and steadily downwards. Several lengths of bandage might be needed.
3 Keep the limb *lower* than the heart.
4 Immobilise the limb by splinting it to a straight branch. Poison flows through the body via the lymphatic system, which uses bodily movement as its pump.
5 Treat the victim for shock. Tell the person that it wasn't a poisonous snake or that most of the venom went outside the wound. If you act calm and collected, chances are the victim's heartbeat will stop racing. This will limit the spread of the venom around the central nervous system until assistance can be sought. Unless you have a stretcher handy, you should not try to move the victim.

Treat spider and scorpion bites much the same way. Keeping the bite area cold helps deaden the pain.

Heat exhaustion

Symptoms of heat exhaustion are a loss of blood in the facial area causing it to turn white and the skin will be wet and cold. If there is a salt deficiency, cramps will also be a symptom. Resting in the shade is the best treatment, followed by drinking water with a pinch of salt in it. If there is no shade available, set up a fly or groundsheet to sit under. Make sure there is adequate ventilation. As in cases of hypothermia, temperature should be restored gradually. Suddenly jumping into icy water can induce shock as blood rushes from one part of the body to another.

The best way to prevent heat exhaustion is to consume plenty of fluids, preferably with some added glucose and salt. See page 71 for additional information. The human body uses water evaporation through the skin to regular temperature, up to 1500 millilitres per hour during strenuous activity. It is therefore necessary to consume at least this amount each hour when climbing.

Hypothermia

Traversing the alpine highlands during a winter storm without adequate clothing is the surest way to get hypothermia. The treatment is to:

- get out of the wind
- replace any wet clothes with dry ones
- put some insulation on the ground
- use a space blanket to reflect internal heat. These blankets can be purchased at most camping shops and even supermarkets and department stores. They contain a layer of reflective foil that insulates body heat very well. Cyclists should always carry such a blanket in cold or alpine conditions.
- eat plenty of food.

Do not drink alcohol as it thins the blood vessels and decreases body temperature. This is a time to become closer to your companions, literally. Shared body warmth can cure all symptoms of hypothermia, but body reserves will still have to be built up after normal body temperature is reached. The best method is by consuming easily ingested sugar, such as sweetened condensed milk.

Sprains

Immobilise the area of the sprain and rest it. Immerse in cold water to lessen the swelling. If applying any pressure is too painful, it could be a fracture and assistance will need to be sought.

Bushfires

If you are threatened by a bushfire while cycling, the worst thing you can do is to panic. Never run uphill or try to outstrip a fire without giving some thought to the situation. Consider the area, the direction of the fire and the wind direction and velocity. When taking action, remember that northern slopes are usually hot and dry and therefore a greater risk area, and that fire burns uphill and is usually most fierce on spurs and ridges.

Do not try to run through a fire front unless it is no wider than 3 metres and no higher than 1.5 metres. Choose the nearest clear space and place an obstruction between yourself and the fire. Quickly clean away all inflammable material, such as leaves and fallen branches. Cover any exposed skin with clothing, preferably wool, and wet if possible. Protect your feet with proper footwear, not thongs, wet any towels, and lie facedown in the clearing. Ensure all skin surfaces are covered; radiant heat from the fire kills, as well as flames. Do not attempt to raise your head too much and so risk inhaling smoke. The freshest air is right next to the ground. If near a deep dam or deep stream, get right into it. Concrete tanks should be avoided as they can explode from the heat. Galvanised or corrugated-iron tanks are also unsuitable because they can buckle and warp, thus allowing the water to escape. Plus the water inside can heat up to boiling point. A large clearing, ravine or gully can also be a good shelter if the fire cannot be outdistanced or outskirted. Wait for the front to pass (which can take as little as 15 minutes), watching out for falling embers. Afterwards, wait for the ground to cool before venturing out from the shelter.

Fitness

Mountain biking is a sport that requires a reasonable level of fitness, despite the fact that the bike does half the work in getting from point A to point B. The reason is that more energy has to be expended per unit of time. Even though a cyclist will require less effort than a walker to complete a trail, the

There is no substitute for an adequate level of fitness.

Refilling a drink bottle in a pristine mountain stream.

cyclist will need a fitter cardiovascular system to sustain a higher rate of energy output as the time taken is significantly less.

Many novices find climbing even gentle hills difficult. This is because at about 85 per cent of your maximum heart rate (on average, 220 minus your age), the body reaches 'the aerobic/anaerobic transition zone', where the lungs are unable to supply a sufficient amount of oxygen to the bloodstream. This means that the body switches over to glycogen to substitute for the deficient oxygen. As a by-product, lactic acid builds up in the muscles. This accumulation quickly reaches a saturation limit within 10 minutes, preventing any further strenuous exertion.

As your fitness increases, the transition zone into the anaerobic state moves closer to the maximum heart rate, preventing the need for lactic acid build-up. At this level, longer periods of high-energy output can be sustained.

As your interest in the sport grows, you will find that regular training at home will increase the enjoyment when out on the trail. A fitter cyclist will need to dismount less often and therefore arrive at the destination sooner. Furthermore, the scenery and thrill of the ride will be more appreciated, rather than being overcome with fatigue or muscle cramp.

Cyclists with specific health conditions such as diabetes, epilepsy, serious allergies or asthma should always take supplies of their required preventative medication. Mountain biking can induce attacks of any of these illnesses.

Outlined here are the four important components to training for achieving fitness for mountain biking.

Specific training goals

There's little point in increasing the weight-lifting ability of your upper arms when the area that specifically needs addressing is cardiovascular endurance. Cycling itself is the best training but this is not always practical and a variety of home rhythmic fitness devices are available that will emulate the same requirements as cycling. In addition to improving overall fitness, you should also work on the hamstrings, calves and thighs in a routine.

Pushing the limits

Progress in fitness is made by pushing the heart and breathing rates to higher levels and sustaining that output for increasingly longer periods. Improving aerobic capacity will strengthen the chambers of the heart so that they are capable of pumping more blood per minute.

Likewise, muscles will be interlaced with more blood vessels and therefore can more efficiently burn oxygen. Another result of regular exercise is that more haemoglobin blood cells are produced which increases the capacity to carry oxygen to the muscles.

Rest

Recovery from high heart rates is very important and your heart rate should be monitored. Recent research into ageing has discovered that a surplus of oxygen actually damages cells and accelerates the ageing process, so it's critical not to overdo it.

Cooling down after a strenuous workout with some light exercise or a massage helps flush out accumulated toxins that have built up during the rapid burning of calories. It also aids the body's future ability to bounce back in ever-shorter periods.

Variety of Exercise

The main reason why people abandon their exercise schedule is lack of interest. Variety will help maintain enjoyment as well as work different muscles in the body. So don't just cycle, do some swimming, walking, jogging or weights.

Nutrition

As mountain biking is a fairly intensive activity with frequent periods of strenuous exertion on uphills and lots of adrenalin coursing through the veins when descending, it is critical to keep blood glucose levels high.

The repetition of pedalling to maintain speed is essentially an aerobic exercise. This energy originates from oxygen, blood glucose and fatty acids. When a hill is encountered and the muscles go into the anaerobic phase, then energy is derived from glycogen. A final, one-off burst-like energy source, located in the muscle cells, is creatine phosphate.

Carbohydrates are the best source of glycogen and ingesting these regularly during a ride can prolong the aerobic phase without having a lactic acid build-up. Carbohydrates are found in fruit, vegetables, potatoes, wholemeal bread, pasta, cereals and rice. They can also be consumed during a ride by drinking specialised sports drinks.

Before commencing an arduous ride, performance can be maximised by eating a high-carbohydrate meal. The timing is critical. If the stomach is still digesting the food when the ride has begun, less blood will be available to the muscles. Consequently, it's wise to complete the meal about three hours before commencing.

Another important consideration is the energy value of each food type. This is measured in calories or kilojoules. A typical mountain bike ride along undulating terrain will burn about 700 calories an hour. The protein content also determines the long-term sustained output, otherwise known as stamina, as opposed to short bursts of energy supplied by glucose-rich foods, such as chocolate.

Food

The table opposite is a list of calorie, carbohydrate and protein content per 100 grams or 100 millilitres of common foods.

Type	Calories (k)	Carbohydrates (g)	Protein (g)
White rice	103	23	2
Beef steak	396	0	26
Chicken	150	0	30
Baked beans	110	21	6
Mushrooms	165	4	3
Potatoes	77	18	2
Apples	55	13	0.4
Cheese	400	0.5	26
Cornflakes	363	79	8
Eggs (2)	150	1	11
Red wine	95	0.5	0.3

Freeze-dried food satchels, such as Alliance, Alpine Aire and Backpackers Pantry, that are commonly found in camping stores are popular for long wilderness expeditions. They are extremely expensive and, despite being reasonable quality, they are not of adequate quantity. For each meal additional food has to be prepared, especially after a long day's cycling. Canned foods and fresh fruit and vegetables are always easy to prepare but should be consumed within the first few days to save weight. For lunches and cold snacks, dried fruit-and-nut mixes give long-lasting nourishment. A quick top-up can be supplied by confectionery.

Drink

For drinks, a little sweetener such as barley sugar in a drink bottle will flavour water. However, mountain streams are quite often so fresh and pure that their taste is entirely different from home tap water and so no sweetener is needed. A problem with sweeteners in drink bottles is that heat will breed fungus in the sugar residue after the first day.

The widely available, colourful isotonic sports drinks are ideally suited to cyclists. They are similar to soft drinks but are not carbonated and contain specific fluid and energy replenishing nutrients such as electrolytes, sodium chloride, potassium and phosphorus, as well as the usual sucrose and glucose.

Added salt helps to prevent cramping. Brand names include Lucozade, Gatorade, Powerade, Isosport, Adams Sport, Energizer and Sports Plus. All these sports drinks are recommended for drinking before, during and after strenuous exercise. The drinks themselves come in plastic containers perfect for throwing in the backpack. Sports scientists tell us that it is beneficial to consume such drinks no more than 45 minutes before the ride. The advice is not to wait until thirst sets in, as by that stage you are already partially dehydrated and fatigued. Therefore, top up every 15–20 minutes when cycling, consuming at least a litre an hour on a hot day. Do this even when you are not immediately thirsty. Some isotonic sports drinks, such as Isosport, come in tablet or powder form. These powder canisters are a handy way to boost energy on long strenuous rides where fresh water is abundant, although you must be careful to clean any containers soon after the ride to remove any sugar residue.

When camping at lookouts, on ridges, plateaus and summits, large supplies of water must be carried, not only for drinking but for cooking and washing. There is no better container than empty plastic soft-drink bottles, which come in a range of sizes and are recyclable, disposable, resealable, flexible, light-weight, cheap and transparent.

Returning from Mt Jagungal, Kosciuszko National Park, New South Wales.

WHERE TO RIDE 7

Environmental impact issues

Mountain bikers have to be on their best behaviour in order to minimise any future hostilities when public land is zoned. Access rights to national parks, State forests and other reserves are fast becoming a contentious issue. Already authorities have prevented the use of walking trails as cycling routes because of the conflict of use and the fragile nature of the trails.

When managers of public land consider which tracks can be made accessible for mountain biking, they are faced with three main information requirements:

- What are the physical impacts of mountain biking upon tracks, facilities, and the environment?
- What are the social impacts of mountain biking upon the other users of tracks and facilities?
- What recreation settings and experiences do mountain bikers prefer?

To date, the discussions and debates associated with mountain biking issues have been mainly confined to subjective magazine articles, anecdotal accounts and advocacy arguments both for and against mountain bike access. However, managers require a more comprehensive and objective research resource to aid their decision-making.

Like any outdoor activity, mountain biking will impact on the environmental conditions present, including the soils, vegetation, water and wildlife. The physical impact of mountain bikes is unique and cannot be categorised with

Authorities recommend going through water as opposed to widening tracks by going around puddles.

motorised vehicles, horses or even walkers. Commonly, mountain bikes are classed together with four-wheel drives and trail bikes through the common element of having wheels. Nothing, of course, could be further from the truth. There are important differences in wheel loadings and power, since mountain bikes are lightweight, non-motorised and have thinner tyres.

Likewise, the effect of cycling on the soils is substantially different from walking. Generally, there are two types of forces exerted on soils by wheels:
● the downwards compaction force due to dynamic load on the wheel
● the rotational shearing stress from the wheel torque acting around the axis.

Mountain bikes will exert downward force through their tyres, although the 'mean ground contact pressure', which comprises the wheel load divided by the contact area, is likely to be less than that of heavier motorised vehicles, horses and heavily laden hikers. With the lower wheel loadings of mountain bikes, their impacts upon downhill slopes are likely to be much less than those from motorbikes. This does assume that the wheels continue to turn rather than skidding with hard braking. Such skidding can loosen track surfaces and move material downhill and, most significantly, promote the development of ruts that channel water-flow.

Such ruts, which can promote erosive water-flows to a greater extent than by footstep puddling, are the most distinctly unique 'wheeling' impact. However, where skidding does not occur, impacts from the normal rolling effects of wheels are less than from walking.

It is off formed trails that these compaction forces will impact on the environment. Most trails are constructed to provide a consolidated and compacted surface, which allows easy travel for users. Where trails are soft and wet, the effect of downward forces will be less a case of compaction and more one of soil smearing and deformation.

Mountain bikes will also exert shearing forces from the torque applied to the rear wheel. When the shear strain of the soil is exceeded, particularly in wet conditions or on unconsolidated surfaces, 'wheel-slip' occurs. Usually, the occurrence of wheel-slip means the cyclist must dismount and walk.

Visitor use surveys

Often at camping grounds and key visitor sites, the national parks authorities place questionnaires called 'Visitor Use Surveys'. These are an important way of letting the authorities know that mountain cyclists use the areas. They ask questions like age of visitors, origins of party, group size, frequency of visits, mode of transport, destination, accommodation, walking/riding intentions, and a request for suggestions. These questionnaires often have an opinion section, asking about attitudes to the popularity of the place, camping restrictions, vehicle access, damage assessment, quality of facilities, and ranger presence. Please take some time to fill these out and take special care to highlight the fact that mountain bikers use the areas.

Code of behaviour

In order to avoid being classified together with motorised transport in any future management policy, some sort of code of ethics should be adopted by commercial tour operators as well as private mountain bikers. The International Mountain Bicycling Association has adopted some simple guidelines based on American experience:

1 Ride on open trails only.
2 Leave no trace.
3 Ride under control.
4 Always yield to others.
5 Never spook animals.
6 Plan ahead.

Here's what mountain biking associations around the globe have established as an off-road cycling code of behaviour:

1 **Self-sufficiency** Carry a first-aid kit and tool set.
2 **Group size** Less than four in a party is considered unsafe, while 10 or more will often lead to rapid track degradation and conflict with other users.
3 **Control** Always ride so one can stop in time for an unexpected reason. Keep the bike well maintained.
4 **Utilitarian rights** Respect the rights of other users such as walkers and equestrians. Because of the silent nature of the bicycle, both walkers and horses are easily startled when a cyclist flies past from behind. Always announce your presence. To avoid spooking horses, dismount and check that the rider is happy for you to pass. Always allow a wide berth.
5 **Weed prevention** Bicycle tyres have been proven to be a cause of the spread of exotic weeds and plant disease by seeds becoming trapped in the tread and dislodging later. Therefore, cleaning the bike regularly not only makes sense for maintenance purposes but also for the environment.
6 **Obeying signs** Some tracks, while perfectly possible to cycle on, are closed to all cyclists because they are being rehabilitated. In general, gazetted wilderness areas involve the closure and revegetation of trails, the erection of barriers, and the implementation of penalties and patrols. While the main perpetrators are four-wheel drivers, mountain biking is not a recreation recognised as being reconcilable with official wilderness areas. Likewise, all walking tracks are out of bounds to bicycles because of the rapid damage to the trail and the conflict of use with walkers. If a walking track must be used, dismount and walk next to the bike.
  Also be aware of the other regulations in regard to total fire bans, camping permits, fees, fuel stove-only areas and rubbish removal. Leave all gates as found.

7 Sensible riding Don't cut corners as this breaks up the soft soil on the shoulders so that the next rain can easily wash it away, leading to erosion. Likewise, skidding accelerates track degradation, especially if the ground is wet. Authorities recommend that cyclists pass through the middle of puddles and mud rather than progressively widening the track by going around them.

Many of these actions will seem to be restrictive, unnecessary or overcautious; however, mountain bikes have already been excluded from large areas of the national parks system. Cyclists are being classified with high-impact users such as trailbikers and four-wheel drivers, rather than low-impact users such as bushwalkers. All major cycling organisations agree there should be no cycling on walking tracks and the provision of facilities at the start of walking tracks to chain-up bikes would be the best way to encourage cyclists not to ride there. Fine examples of the implementation of this policy are prevalent on Lord Howe Island.

Touring

The best method for planning a route is to purchase maps covering the designated area and trace out a route along the vehicular tracks that follow the most scenic way to the destination. The distance of the trail can be measured in centimetres with a piece of string. On the popular 1:25,000 topographical maps, simply divide the length of the string by four to obtain the distance of the journey in kilometres. One can also purchase a simple mechanical gadget called a 'map meter' that can be rolled along the intended route and will give the horizontal distance. Map meters are available at most camping stores. Either way, you simply add on 20–30 per cent to account for altitudinal fluctuations to give a conservative estimate of the distance.

While there are wide fluctuations in a mountain biker's speed (anything from 4 km/h walking up a hill to 60 km/h flying down the other side), the average sustained cycling speed on a dirt trail through moderately hilly country is about 7–10 km/h. Therefore, don't try to plan day trips longer than about 50 kilometres unless the terrain is predominantly downhill, especially if laden with panniers. This will leave plenty of time for rest breaks, sightseeing, walking side trips and unexpected delays. Ridge and plateau riding is the fastest as a good momentum can be maintained both ways. Cyclists travelling for many days will find that their fitness increases over the duration of the excursion and distances on the last day can be more easily accomplished than on the first day. Having less to carry also helps. Very rough tracks, steep hills and navigational errors will reduce a cyclist's average speed in mountainous country to that of walking, and sometimes even slower.

The best and simplest tip one can follow is to leave early, at around 6 or 7 o'clock in the morning. If everything goes according to plan then the destination is reached early. If things don't, there's still time to deal with problems. One of the main problems with mountain bike touring is running out of daylight hours.

Learn to recognise features on the map by using the contour lines (lines that join places of equal height). This will allow you to check your progress. Orthodox navigation skills involving conversion of bearings and resection are totally unnecessary. Simply familiarise yourself with how contour lines represent the landscape. After a few trips in the wilderness, you should be able to recognise simple and common features on the map, such as mountains, valleys, ridgelines, saddles and cliffs.

Cycling computers enable you to monitor your progress and confirm your position. When calibrated correctly, they are amazingly accurate.

Code of behaviour when camping

Much of the camping code of behaviour is common sense. Studies into the effects of camping have concluded that the following practices should be adhered to:

- Washing dishes and bathing should be done at least 50 metres from streams as soap, detergents and food scraps are all harmful to aquatic life. Biodegradable organic soaps are preferable to commercial chemical-based varieties.
- Human waste should be well buried (at least 15 centimetres deep) with the use of a trowel, at least 100 metres from streams. This reduces the incidence of gastroenteritis caused by exposed faecal matter. Gastro and giardia (human bacterial parasites) exist in watercourses contaminated by faecal waste. The parasites are fairly common in popular camping sites in New Zealand, the United States and Europe, and have recently spread to Australia. The most prone areas are in alpine regions. Symptoms of infection include severe diarrhoea and vomiting that can last a month. Always use a pit toilet if they're provided. Some camping stores now

With a mountain bike, your next destination is limited only by the extent of your own imagination and information on interesting places to visit.

import heavy-duty sealable bags for carrying out human waste—drastic measures for particularly sensitive areas. Camp at low-impact sites at least 30 metres away from watercourses. Sand and hard surfaces are better than wet, soft, boggy or vegetated areas. Choose pre-existing campsites rather than clearing a new one. This can be achieved by planning ahead.

● The use of modern tents is encouraged. Pitched properly they are mostly waterproof and don't require the digging of perimeter trenches. They come with fibreglass or aluminium frames so saplings do not need to be cut down for poles, and foam or inflatable mats make obsolete the traditional practice of cutting fern fronds for bedding.

● Carry all rubbish out. Remove the ends off tins and flatten. Remember that animals can dig up buried rubbish.

● Where fires are allowed, use existing fireplaces. Do not encircle them with rocks. Use only fallen dead wood. Don't use your fire as a rubbish tip and extinguish it completely before you leave. Water is preferable to sand to extinguish flames.

- Keep group sizes to a minimum of four to eight cyclists.
- Spread out in open untracked country rather than riding single file, so the impact on vegetation is minimised. A plant trampled on once has more of a chance of surviving. Keep on rocks where possible.
- Wear lightweight boots with soft rubber compound soles rather than heavy-duty army ones.
- Choose a different route each time when visiting a trackless area, and try to camp at different sites whenever possible.

Touring in Australia

At first glance, Australia might not seem like a good prospect for mountain biking, because it doesn't have any really huge mountains. It's the flattest continent on Earth. As the essential ingredient of a quality off-road ride is a good downhill, places such as the Nullarbor Plain would have difficulty in qualifying.

Besides the art of utilising gravity, other criteria for 'class' off-road action include the number and diversity of trails, ease of accessibility, and the area's scenic value. For these reasons, this book focuses on the best areas for mountain biking in south-eastern Australia.

Although fine mountain bike touring regions can also be found in Western Australia, South Australia and the Northern Territory, the Great Dividing Range that runs from the Grampians in western Victoria to Cape York in northern Queensland provides the most opportunities for exploiting differences in altitude.

In terms of overnight expeditions, each State's national parks policy on camping is decentralised, with regional headquarters imposing their own regulations depending on the specifics of the area. In some parks, such as Lake Eildon in Victoria, fees will apply at certain areas, and restrictions on aspects such as fireplaces and length of stay are enforced. These camping grounds require advance booking, especially during school holidays.

In Queensland, popular parks such as Mount Barney have restrictions on the maximum numbers of visitors per campsite . By contrast, the Wollemi National Park wilderness in New South Wales has very limited use and you can camp wherever you want.

In higher alpine areas, such as above the treeline (1700 metres) in Kosciuszko National Park, throughout Tasmania's World Heritage Parks and in most of the country's officially declared wilderness, campers must observe a fuel-stove only policy. These areas are declared environmentally sensitive regions where campfires have been banned because of the past effects of bushfires, often started by out-of-control campfires. For example, in Tasmania since 1960, 16 per cent of alpine flora and 8 per cent of rainforest have been burnt. Several of the species that grow in these areas, such as Huon pine, King Billy pine, pencil pine and deciduous beech, do not regenerate. Huts located in the World Heritage Area now have coal supplied for heating.

Banning campfires and the imposition of a hefty penalty also reduces the likelihood of native trees being cut down for wood, which expands small clearings into larger ones and leaves visual scarring. Furthermore, many people use fires as a rubbish place. Since impractically large, intense fires are needed to disintegrate tins, cans and bottles, park rangers have often found campsites left with a lot of half-burnt rubbish.

The Tasmanian bush, with its high winter rainfall and drying summer winds, is especially susceptible to ignition. The people of Hobart discovered this in 1967 when a wall of fire swept around Mount Wellington and destroyed homes, businesses and 51 lives. Over the last two decades there have been numerous cases of campfire escapes. These fires often have

Forest scenery in Cape Otway National Park, Victoria.

Overlooking the Megalong Valley, Blue Mountains, New South Wales.

the heat intensity to enter rainforest and wetland areas. The peat soils that cover extensive areas of western Tasmania are particularly vulnerable to fire. Peat is made up of decomposed, compressed organic matter. It is dark, greasy, and feels springy if walked on. Fires can burn down into the soil and smoulder for months, thus serving as potential ignition sources during hot, dry weather.

The onus is on cyclists to make themselves aware of the various regulations. These can usually be obtained at the local ranger station. Today, the internet is increasingly popular for disseminating government policies and management plans. Newsgroups on cycling, walking and camping also discuss much relevant information about these issues.

The Blue Mountains

This massive dissected sandstone plateau forms the western boundary of Sydney and extends almost 300 kilometres from Mittagong in the south to Denman in the north. The newly proposed World Heritage Area is comprised of seven national parks: Blue Mountains, Wollemi, Kanangra Boyd, Thirlmere Lakes, Nattai, Gardens of Stone and Goulburn River. The Blue Mountains contain outstanding landscapes including rugged cliff-lined escarpments, beautiful lakes, dramatic gorges, wild rivers, deep narrow canyons, and vast uncompromised natural areas.

Mountain bike enthusiasts have numerous trails to explore, many of which are closed to four-wheel drives. By combining cycling with walking, they can penetrate deep into the heart of the wilderness for that magic outdoors experience. By using the hourly rail service that crosses the Blue Mountains, cyclists only sore muscles will be in their braking hands.

The Australian Alps

The area spanning the Great Dividing Range peaks in northern Victoria (Alpine National Park) and New South Wales (Kosciuszko National Park) forms the Australian Alps, large tracts of which are snowbound in winter.

Despite their high altitude, many of the inclines in the alps are moderate and well graded. There is plenty of variety offered, from exploration potential for hard-core bikers to gentle, family day excursions. Their rich grazing heritage and hydro-electric schemes have left a legacy of trails. The lack of vegetation above the treeline allows superb views and descents can be as long as 1500 metres.

Tasmanian World Heritage Area

The south-western quarter of Tasmania offers one of the highest quality and best-loved wilderness regions on the planet. National parks include the mighty South West, Mount Field and Franklin–Gordon Wild Rivers, and Cradle Mountain–Lake St Clair. Tall jagged quartzite peaks sawtooth the panoramic horizon and majestic forests with some of the world's tallest, oldest and rarest plants are all attractions. Due to the fragility and importance of this special region, camping and fire restrictions apply to visitors and cyclists are confined to only a few major trails. There is minimal traffic, however, so mountain bikers do not have to share the experience with hordes of tourists.

East Gippsland

East Gippsland lies between the Great Dividing Range and the coast in Australia's south-east corner. The crescent between Eden in New South Wales and Sale in Victoria offers the best coastal cycling in the country. The proximity of mountains and ocean offers the ultimate in variety for off-road adventurers. Numerous national parks, nature reserves and State forests riddled with many logging trails are ideal for out-of-the way cycling. Distances are vast—this is the stuff of long, epic expeditions.

The Brindabellas

Only a few minutes' drive from Canberra, the Brindabellas form the western boundary of the Australian Capital Territory. Rising to over 1800 metres, they regularly attract snowfalls. Because of the many steep kilometre-long descents, easy vehicular access, and great views over Canberra and Kosciuszko, the Brindabellas are a popular destination for weekend mountain biking.

Queensland's Scenic Rim

Surrounding Brisbane and bordering New South Wales, a great volcanic range hosts a variety of tropical vegetation and a dramatic uplifted escarpment.

Numinbah Valley viewed from Queensland's Lamington National Park.

Queenslanders own more mountain bikes per person than in any other State, and the scenic rim is their favourite playground. Access is easy, well developed facilities are nearby, and trails are firm and well maintained. Car shuttles help avoid those long, arduous hills.

The Grampians (Gariwerd National Park)

In central western Victoria lies a heavily tilted sandstone plateau comprised of three major sections. The tourist town of Halls Gap is the main entrance and facilities cater for all types of visitors. Despite the banning of mountain bikes on many of the park's management trails there remains ample opportunity to explore the maze of fascinating eroded formations. The abundance of wildlife is a renowned attraction of this semi-arid region.

The Budawangs

The southern New South Wales towns of Milton and Nerriga lie on the doorstep to some of the wildest terrain in eastern Australia. Primarily located in Morton National Park, the Budawangs have long been a mecca for wilderness enthusiasts. Whether it's the coastal views from the messa-like plateaus, or the grandiose Clyde River gorge, the Budawangs are extremely spectacular for mountain biking. Self-sufficiency in these mountains is paramount.

Lord Howe Island

Located east of Port Macquarie, about halfway between New Zealand and the Australian mainland, Lord Howe is a small mountainous island of unparalleled beauty. Two massive mountains dominate the tiny island, all of which is a World Heritage Area. Cycling is the main form of transport on the island, much of which is in a natural state, with development and tourism strictly curtailed. Access is by air from Sydney and bikes can be hired.

The Otways

The Great Ocean Road in south-western Victoria lines one of the most rugged coastlines in the world. The hinterland, between Anglesea and Port Fairy, is a paradise of undulating hills, waterfalls and dense rainforest. Despite relatively close proximity to Melbourne, mountain bikers are rewarded with a natural escape offering a diverse range of topography. The Otways are primarily wet coastal ranges with an excellent network of fire trails and management tracks.

Queenstown and the Remarkables mountain range on the South Island.

Touring in New Zealand

Most of New Zealand's population of 3.5 million can be found in the country's five largest cities. Outside of these cities are numerous mountains and lakes that form idyllic cycling territory. It was in the mid-1980s that mountain biking became prevalent and now has become a fully commercial activity to the extent of employing helicopters to shuttle the keen downhill enthusiast to high-altitude staging areas. Because of this popularity, off-road cycling now represents probably the most significant new-use issue facing managers of outdoor recreation areas. The main challenge for managers has been to determine how mountain biking fits into the range of recreation opportunities they currently provide. The Department of Conservation and many other public land managers, such as local authorities, recognise mountain biking as a legitimate form of outdoor recreation and have specifically zoned and advertised certain trails for the use of cyclists. Mountain bikes are only permitted on maintained roads, however, so even abandoned four-wheel tracks are off-limits.

Te Wahipounamu

The majestic World Heritage Area of Te Wahipounamu in the South Island is made up of four national parks: Fiordland, Mount Aspiring, Westland and

Mount Cook. The weather is often very cold and wet but the scenery is sublime. The popular staging areas for facilities, supplies and accommodation are Te Anau, Queenstown, Glenorchy and Wanaka.

Nelson

Nelson is at the northern end of New Zealand's South Island, encompassing the substantial Kahurangi as well as the Mount Richmond Forest Park.

The variety in terrain, alternating between coast and mountains, offers plenty for the self-sufficient, experienced mountain biker willing to carry provisions. Much of the northern part of the South Island is sparsely populated. One of the highlights is the Rameka Track in the Abel Tasman National Park.

Volcanic regions

The volcanic regions lie in the centre of the North Island, between Rotorua and Wanganui. Spectacular mountain biking opportunities can be found in the Tongariro National Park, which is centred on the three major volcanic peaks of Tongariro, Ngauruhoe and Ruapehu. Like Fiordland, this is also a World Heritage Area, but has substantial facilities. Despite the high altitude, access is available all year round.

Returning from Ben Lomond on the South Island.

Cycling sites in south-eastern Australia

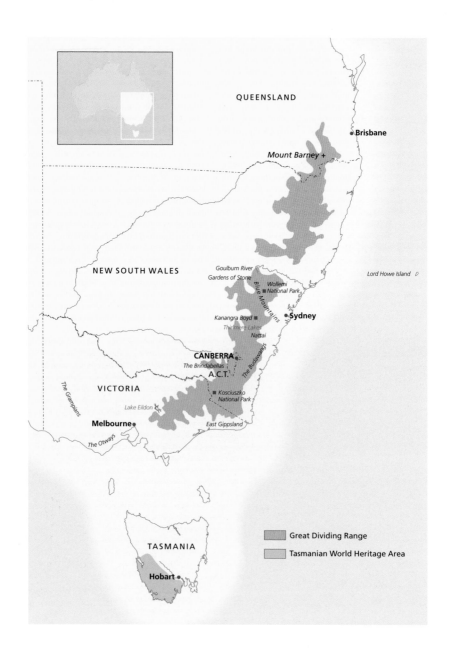

Cycling sites in New Zealand

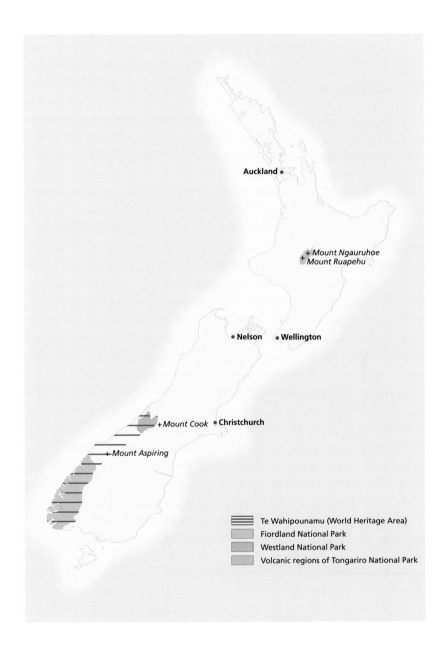

Mountain Biking and Cycling Organisations

AUSTRALIA

National organisations

Australian Mountain Bike Association
A body generally concerned with administration of mountain biking at a national level. Is involved with competitive events.
AMBA
c/- Australian Cycling Federation
14 Telopea Avenue
Homebush NSW 2140

Mountain Bike Access Australia
Formed in response to a small but growing number of trail closures in Australia, the objectives of this body are to:
● represent the interests of mountain bikers
● promote equitable and environmentally sustainable trail access
● inform and educate for safe and responsible bike use of trails
● work with other user groups on issues of trail access.
The MBAA also aims to educate land managers about the true impact of mountain bikes.

For further information contact:
Stuart McDougall, President MBAA
Phone: (02) 9327 8344
Fax: (02) 9363 4597

Note Most clubs are run by volunteers, and committee members are often appointed short-term, so contact details here may become outdated quickly. The local cycle shop is probably the best place to find out about clubs in the area.

State organisations

The clubs listed below organise social rides on weekends. Some hold races at various levels. Updated contact phone numbers and addresses can be found in a current issue of *Australian Mountain Biking* magazine. Many clubs also have a home page on the internet.

AUSTRALIAN CAPITAL TERRITORY
Canberra Off Road Cyclists
Tony Scott: (02) 6249 3573
email: corstuff@hotmail.com

NEW SOUTH WALES
Australian Bush Cycle Touring Association
Sue Webber: (02) 4464 2316
Banana Coast All Terrain Cycles
Wally Sims: (02) 6653 3692
Central Coast Cycling Club
Dave Gibson: (02) 4393 1511
Hunter Valley
Brian Butler: (02) 4945 3517
Muswellbrook Cycle Club
Tony Hernando: (02) 6545 3140
Nowra Velo Club
Doug Holland: (02) 4421 7094
Razorback Bangers Mountain Bike Club
Alison Scambury: (02) 4684 2291
Southern Off Road Cycling Club
Paul Dreghorn: (02) 9520 1045
email: kcyc@one.net.au
Western Sydney Mountain Bike Club
Frank van Zanten: (02) 4735 7872
Brad Payne: (02) 4751 1928
Wollongong Mountain Bike Club
Alan Boyle: (02) 4284 2564

NORTHERN TERRITORY

Alice Springs Mountain Biking Club
Charlie Lawrence: (041) 889 7508

Crazy Dog Road and Mountain Bike Club, Katherine
Mark McIntosh: (08) 8972 1213 (BH)
or (08) 8971 7475 (AH)
website: www.crazydog.com.au

QUEENSLAND

Bayside Hillbillies Mountain Bike Club
Cycle City Cleveland: (07) 3821 2801

Bundy Bats Mountain Bike Club
Jenny & Bevan Roberts: (07) 4152 6717

Bushrangers Mountain Bike Club Sunshine Coast Inc.
Troy Zwart: (07) 5448 0858

Cairns Mountain Bike Club
Barbara Meade: (07) 4054 2350
Dan Foley: (07) 4054 5492

Club Bikeline
Damien McCottor: (07) 4638 2242

Cycledelic
Ray Pope: (07) 3371 5364

North Brisbane Mountain Bike Club
Dale Garvey: (07) 3351 4597

Queensland Cyclists Association
Nigel Walker: (07) 3390 1477
email: qca@gil.com.au

Rocky Mountain Bikers Mountain Bike Club
Gordon Burkhardt: (07) 4928 4207

The Riders Club
Pete Smith: (07) 3352 7772
email: webmaster@trc.org.au

SOUTH AUSTRALIA

Adelaide Mountain Bike Club
Scott Keneally: (019) 670 302
email: info@ambc.mtx.net

Bicycle South Australia
Cormac McCarthy: (08) 8410 1406

Inside Line Mountain Bike Club
Garry Patterson: (015) 791 541

Gawler MBX Club
Peter Herriman: (08) 8522 4850
email: peter@dove.net.au
website: www.dove.net.au/
  ~peterh/gmbx/welcome.htm

TASMANIA

Diet Devils
John De Vries: (03) 6228 6887

Launceston City Cycling Club
Robyn Bailey: (03) 6343 1125

North West Mountain Bikes
Andrew Nichols: (03) 6425 5223

VICTORIA

Albury-Wodonga Mountain Bike Club
Darryl Dear: (02) 6024 4605

Alpine Cycling Club
Gary Meyland: (03) 5756 2403

Extreme Mountain Bike Club
Eric Chan: (03) 9817 2245

Fat Tyre Flyers
Andrew Johns: (0418) 502 273

GASP (Gippsland)
Lenny Van Berkel: (03) 5192 4462

Melbourne Premier Cycling Club
Jason Lowder: (0412) 269 714
email: jasonlowder@csse.monash.edu.au

MUDCRABS
Martin Tobin: (02) 6032 9434

WESTERN AUSTRALIA

Claremont/Nedlands Mountain Bike Club
Phil Harris: (08) 9386 3792

Perth Mountain Bike Club
Infoline: (08) 9487 6221

South West Mountain Bike Club
Barrie Thomas: (08) 9721 8924

Spokes Mountain Bikers
Darryl Shields: (08) 9964 1399

NEW ZEALAND

National organisation

**The New Zealand Mountain
Bike Association**
This association was formed in 1989 to:
• promote and represent the interests
  of all mountain bikers in New Zealand
• encourage mountain biking as a
  recreational and competitive sport
• promote off-road code of behaviour
• promote protection and preservation
  of New Zealand's natural environment
• organise/sanction mountain bike
  events.
Members receive a regular newsletter,
discount entry to sanctioned events
and representation at land management meetings.

For more information contact the local
mountain bike club or write to:

NZMBA Secretary
PO Box 361
Timaru
Phone/Fax: (03) 686 0975
www.mountainbike.co.nz/nzmba

There is a good general website listing
many of the mountain biking clubs
in New Zealand. It also provides a
search function for mountain biking
information. Check out the website:
www.mountainbike.co.nz

Regional organisations

**Canterbury University Mountain
Bike Club**
Stuart Newmarch: (03) 348 9332
email: san42@student.canterbury.ac.nz
PO Box 9287, Christchurch

Counties Manukau (Auckland)
Natasha Freeman: (09) 527 4135
5/1 Mountainview Mews,
Mt Wellington, Auckland

Hamilton Mountain Bike Club
James Gurney: (07) 854 1498
PO Box 1113, Hamilton

Mountain Biking Otago
Mike Anderson: (03) 477 9494
email: pete.mcdonald@clear.net.nz
PO Box 5913, Dunedin

Rotorua Mountain Bike Club
Mike Stead: (07) 362 8678
mikestead@clear.net.nz
21b Tarawera Rd, Rotorua

Southland MTB
Gary McKenzie: (03) 218 1292
5/201 Tweed St, Invercargill

**Wellington Mountain Bike and
Cycle Touring Club**
Steve White: (06) 306 8007
email: essandsee@extra.co.nz
PO Box 76 Martinborough

Whakatipu Cycle
Gary Steadman: (03) 442 3790
PO Box 484, Queenstown

FURTHER READING

General mountain biking books

The Australian Bicycle Book: Maintenance and Riding Skills
John Harland (Penguin, 1992)
The Fat Tire Rider
Kennedy, *et al*, (Vitesse Press, 1993)
The Mountain Bike Book
David Leslie (Ward Lock, 1996)
The Mountain Bike Handbook,
Barry Ricketts, (The Arena Press, 1988)
A Complete Book of All-Terrain Bicycle
Eugene Sloane (Fireside, 1985)
Mountain Bikes: Maintenance & Repair
John Stevenson (Bicycle Books, 1992)
The Mountain Bike Book
Rod van der Plas, (Bicycle Books, 1989)
Mountain Bike Maintenance
Rod van der Plas, (Bicycle Books, 1995)

Touring in Australia

Cycling the Bush, a series by Sven Klinge (Hill of Content, 1991-99), are the most comprehensive mountain bike guide books available, containing maps, colour photographs and track notes to the best wilderness regions.
Jim Smith's *Guide to the Blue Mountains* (1980) was among the first modern-day books that dealt with off-road touring in the country.
Over the last five years, a profusion of touring guides have been published.

The best cycling publications shop is Bicycle New South Wales, located at Level 2, 209 Castlereagh Street, Sydney. They stock the following good publications:
Cycling Around Sydney with Hang-Ten (Bicycle NSW). A guide to rides around the Sydney metropolitan area.

Cycling Around Grafton and Clarence Valley (Craig Bellamy). A localised guide covering 16 rides in northern NSW.

Cycling the Southern Highlands and South Coast of NSW (Richard Henderine). Covers 30 rides in northern Morton National Park.

Riding Canberra's Bike Paths (Graeme Barrow). Covers the best of the 150 kilometres of bike paths in Canberra.

40+ Bicycle Rides Around Canberra and Southern NSW (Pedal Power ACT). This best-selling guide has 44 touring bike rides and several mountain bike rides, including exploration of the Brindabellas.

Discovering NSW Rainforests: Touring, Walking and Cycling (Total Environment Centre). A small section covers easy, extended tours of the northern national parks.

The Pacific Bicycle Route (Bicycle Australia). Describes cycling conditions between Brisbane and Sydney.

The Blue Mountains: A Guide for Bicyclists (Jim Smith). Covers 48 graded rides in the Blue Mountains.

Bicycle Touring in Australia (Leigh Hemmings). Features eight rides in Australia, (an average of one per State)

Seeing Sydney by Bicycle (Julia Thorn). An extended version of the BINSW/Hang-Ten publication.

Bicycle Tours of South-eastern Australia (Julia Thorn). Covers five extended touring bike rides in rural NSW.

Mountain Bike Trails of the Snowys Vols I & II (Gavin Scott). A guide to 17 great off-road rides.

Pedalling Around Southern Queensland (Julia Thorn). Focuses on general touring.

Bicycling Around Victoria (Ray Pearce). Over 50 day and weekend rides.

Touring in New Zealand

Classic New Zealand Mountain Bike Rides 4th ed. (P, S and J Kennett). 400 rides in 352 pages—the definitive bible of New Zealand Mountain biking. Route descriptions are brief and each major ride has an elevation profile chart.

The following titles focus on general road touring in New Zealand:

New Zealand by Bike (Bruce Ringer)

North Island Pedallers Paradise (Nigel Rushton)

South Island Pedallers Paradise (Nigel Ruston)

Magazines

Cycling magazines are a great source of up-to-date information. A list of cycling club addresses are a standard inclusion.

Australian-based cycling magazines:

Australian Mountain Bike (monthly). Dedicated to off-road cycling exclusively. Independent, usage-based coverage of bikes and mountain bike-related products, racing coverage, riding stories and high-quality repair and maintenance information.

Bicycling Australia (monthly). Of interest to cyclists and bicycle retailers in Australia and New Zealand.

Australian Cyclist (bi-monthly). Of interest to both cyclists and bicycle retailers within Australia and New Zealand. Available by subscription.

Magazines of international interest:

Bicycle Industry News (issued quarterly). Independent coverage of events, shows and news from industry and enthusiast associations.

Encycleopedia (annually, by subscription). Features on some of the most unusual, exotic bicycles on Earth. Out standing photography and editorials.

Bicycling Trade (issued quarterly). A trade-only publication aimed squarely at the needs of bicycle retailers.

Bike Culture (quarterly, by subscription). Covers various aspects of cycling with local and global relevance. Web site at http://bikeculture.com/home/

Bicycle Forum (quarterly, by subscription) A publication of the Bicycle Federation of America (BFA).

Cycle Press (11 issues per year). The only international bicycle industry publication. It's read by more industry leaders than any other trade paper.

Cycle Trader / Cycle Press (issued monthly). Covers the UK industry, products and events .

Glossary

A brief glossary of technical terms associated with mountain biking:

ATB All-terrain bike (also mountain bike or fat-tyre bike).

Bottom bracket A flexible bottom bracket reduces efficiency as pedal power is wasted in moving the bottom of the frame from side to side.

Bottom bracket height This is the height from the centre of the crankcase to the ground. If intending to do a lot of off-road riding in rough conditions, buy a bike that maximises this height so that the chainwheel or pedals don't scrape every time a small crest or rock is passed over.

Cantilever brakes A very efficient braking system whereby two brakepads are mounted by pivots to the frame and contracted by means of an anchor plate connected to a centre-pull cable.

Chrome molybdenum tubing An alloy (531/653) of chrome, molybdenum, manganese, carbon, silicon, sulphur and phosphorus. This is the most common type of steel alloy in the frame. Even though it is lighter, it's actually stronger than steel. In general, the thinner the grade, the higher the cost. But not all of the bike will necessarily be made from chromoly: for the down-market models the forks and rear triangle are sometimes made from high-tensile steel (1020) as a sneaky cost-cutting measure. New materials include aluminium, carbon fibre, titanium, magnesium metal matrix and even plastic! These are the bikes of the future with total weights as low as 9 kilograms.

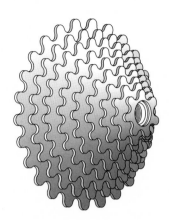

The rear cluster.

Clusters This is the group of six to nine gears on the rear wheel. Also referred to as a cassette or sprocket cluster. The market standards are Shimano's HG and IG range that can handle changing gears even under pressure. Previously this would have meant the chain coming off and maybe breaking but this remarkable gear system handles the stress considerably well. Seven gears were standard for a long time but recently eight- and nine-speed clusters are become popular, not necessarily giving a wider range of gears but allowing smoother shifts. The use of new alloys has cancelled out weight gains by adding gear cogs.

Double-butted tubing The thickness of the frame's tubing varies from being relatively thin at the middle, to thick at the ends. It is primarily used to manufacture lightweight bikes but the weight saving comes at a rigidity cost.

Drop-outs This refers to the rear triangle assembly where the wheel is secured to the frame. If one has to push the wheel forward to remove it, it is called a horizontal drop-out, or if the

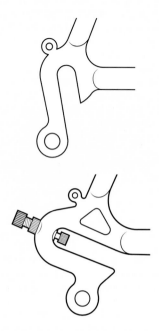

Vertical and horizontal drop-outs.

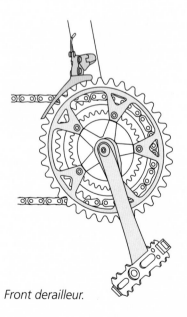

Front derailleur.

wheel can be pulled straight down after removing the nut, it is a vertical drop-out. The latter has the advantage of better wheel alignment, while the former allows for superior gear adjustment.

Front derailleur This is the device that changes the chain's position on the three front chain rings. Changing up gears in the front is the most difficult of all the bike's operations as this involves greatest shifting distance and the most amount of energy.

Gripshift Originating in the United States in early 1994, gripshift employs a simple twisting system similar to motorbikes and is essentially part of the handle grip. There are many models that vary in smoothness and distance of turn to shift the display. The advantages of gripshift are:

- Lightweight and simple, have fewer parts and are easier to work with.
- Maintenance free. Applying a little special-purpose gripshift grease every few months is all that's required.
- Extreme shifts. Go from top to bottom in one easy twist.
- Easy to use. Numbered displays give immediate feedback.

The disadvantages are:

- Unwanted shifting. Rough, rocky trails can sometimes provoke an involuntary shift.
- Ride security. Shifting requires a loosening of the grip on the bars that can be dangerous if negotiating a particularly technical section.
- No braking whilst shifting. It is difficult to turn the wrist and brake. properly at the same time.
- Shortened handlebar grips. There is less room on the handlebars for bar-ends.

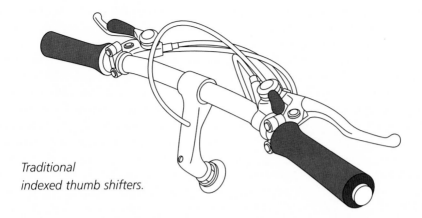

Traditional
indexed thumb shifters.

Indexed gears Like a digital clock, what indexing basically entails is an accurate and reliable means of changing gears as a click and a discrete stop represent the selected gear. Pushing the shifter one click changes the gear by one cog. It's as simple as that.

Some different systems are available. These include rapidfire, traditional thumb shifters and gripshift. Top models include the Shimano XT and XTR.

The new generation of indexed gears might even use a power-assisted electrical mechanism to change gear selection that promises even smoother, more reliable changes.

MTB Mountain bike (also all-terrain bike, fat-tyre bike).

Quick-release These have been the standard in racing bikes for years and have only recently ventured on to mountain bike frames. What is referred to is a small lever that replaces the bolt on the seat and wheels so they can be easily removed. This means that changing a tyre can be done in less time, as can changing the seat height for different gradients. A quick-release lever on top of the seat post allows one to quickly adjust the angle of the seat. Testing has confirmed there is no loss of safety when riding off-road. The disadvantage is that theft of the wheels and seat is made easier. Some of the up-market brakes also have quick-release capabilities so that tubes do not have to be deflated to remove the wheel.

Rapidfire The introduction of rapidfire 'push-button' gears in the early 1990s enjoyed initial success. In its initial

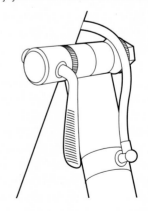

Quick-release lever.

stage, both up and down levers were activated by the thumb under the handlebar. The two levers sat atop one another and were not much of an improvement on the thumb shifters they replaced. The only improvement was that the lever didn't need to be pushed to another position, just press it and it sprang back. This was meant to be a quicker system, hence the name. In reality, though, it wasn't.

In 1993, the second-generation rapidfire plus was introduced, having a wishbone two lever thumb and pointer finger combination. This system had the following advantages:

- Ergonomic. It followed the natural movements of the fingers when gripping the handlebar.
- Practical. Assigning shifting up (larger cogs on the back, smaller cogs on the front) to the stronger thumb and shifting down to the pointer finger was easy to learn and worked well.
- Quick. Upshifts come three at a time and downshifts come with a really light flick of the pointer finger.
- Smooth. The matched Shimano systems work very smoothly together, although earlier systems did lose their spring tension.
- Safe. The rapidfire plus allows shifting whilst braking.

The disadvantages are:

- Complexity. Rapidfire plus is difficult to repair.
- Less componentry. Flexibility as brake levers are often included.
- Breakable. The mechanisms and levers can be fragile if abused.
- No extreme shifting is possible. Down-shifts have to be one click at a time.

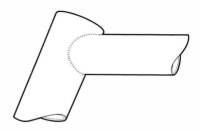

TIG-welded lugless joint.

TIG-welded lugless joints The majority of mountain bike frames are made of tubes that were welded together using this method. In order to prevent corrosion, the electrical welding is conducted in an inert argon-gas atmosphere. The joints are made less abrupt by applying a polyester spackling compound. Other joining methods include brass brazing with lugs and fillet brazing (no lugs).

Index